Accounts of the
Battle of Austerlitz

Napoleon at the Battle of Austerlitz

Accounts of the Battle of Austerlitz

Four perspectives of Napoleon's Campaign of 1805

ILLUSTRATED

K. Stutterheim, Montgomery B. Gibbs, J. H. Henderson and Louis-François Lejeune

Accounts of the Battle of Austerlitz
Four perspectives of Napoleon's Campaign of 1805
K. Stutterheim, Montgomery B. Gibbs, J.H. Henderson and
Louis- François Lejeune

ILLUSTRATED

FIRST EDITION

Leonaur is an imprint of Oakpast Ltd
Copyright in this form © 2023 Oakpast Ltd

ISBN: 978-1-916535-00-8 (hardcover)
ISBN: 978-1-916535-01-5 (softcover)

http://www.leonaur.com

Publisher's Notes

The views expressed in this book are not necessarily those of the publisher.

Contents

A Detailed Account of the Battle of Austerlitz *By K. Stutterheim*	7
To the Public	9
To the Austrian Army	13
Introduction	15
March of the Combined Army into the Position of Olmutz	22
Offensive Movements of the Allied Army	28
Battle of Austerlitz	44
The 3rd and 4th of December	76
Ulm and Austerlitz *By Montgomery B. Gibbs*	83
A Synopsis of the Austerlitz Campaign *By J. H. Henderson*	123
Lejeune's Experiences at Austerlitz *By Louis François Lejeune*	129

Tou cela, prouve, qu'il y a beaucoup d'hommes, capables de faire manoeuvrer, quinze a ving mille hommes, et qu'il en est peu, qui puissent tirer tout le parti possible, d'une armée de quatre-vingt mille hommes.
Note par un officier François

To the Public

The fatal consequences that resulted from the Battle of Austerlitz, to the cause of Europe, and of humanity, render it an object of too deep an interest with the statesman and the soldier to make an apology requisite for introducing to the public, what may be considered as the Austrian official account of that action. It is hardly probable, that, under a government so constituted as that of Austria, a general officer would have ventured to publish the particulars of an action, in which he himself bore a conspicuous part, (at least with his name attached to it,) unless he felt himself sanctioned by the *highest authority* in so doing.

However, that may be, the work bears evident internal marks of authenticity, while the events daily passing under our eyes, with such dazzling, and unprecedented rapidity, give an additional interest to the cause which has been productive of such direful effects.

Scarcely have twelve months elapsed since this disastrous battle was fought, and already have we seen new dynasties created, and the proudest empires levelled in the dust.

We have seen one of the most powerful monarchies of Europe, whether it be considered as to its military resources, or its well replenished treasury; as to its well-disciplined army, or the glorious recollection of its past achievements: we have seen the Armies of Prussia, which were wont to be considered as the patterns of military excellence, dissipated and annihilated, like chaff before the wind, by the well-trained legions of the modern Alexander.

The present state of Europe affords ample scope to the reflections of the statesman. For, though the soldier may account for the loss of a battle, by reasoning on what was done, and what was left undone, the subjugation of states is to be looked for in causes far remote from the scene of action. These are times which not only require superiority of intellect in those who govern, but the conviction on the part of the *governed*, that they are not mere spectators of the fray; that it is not a mere squabble for power; but that the happiness of each individual, that the preservation of all he holds most dear, in short, that the *liberties of his country* are at stake, and depend upon the issue of the contest.

Has this been, or *could it be*, the feeling of those nations of the Continent we have seen overrun?

In the answer to this simple question, we may perhaps find the *real* cause of all the disasters of the coalition, and subject of much contemplation for ourselves. The cloud which has been long gathering over Europe has begun to burst; we have seen the storm fall where least expected, and bury whole empires, and their people, in one common ruin. When the demon of destruction is abroad, let us not be unmindful of ourselves. Are we better prepared than our neighbours? Have we more skilful generals, or less intriguing politicians? I fear not. It is then only to the people we can look in the day of trial; and I trust there is yet enough left of the genuine spirit of the constitution, and of the native valour of Britons, to make every man feel his country is worth contending for. *The moment that ceases to be the case, our independence as a nation is virtually gone*; and, though our empire may drag on a precarious existence for a few years, it will fall, inevitably fall, at no distant period.

I have been inadvertently led into a train of reflection, which some persons may think not quite compatible with the character of a soldier. Against this opinion, I beg leave to enter my protest. I have always considered the superiority of the French troops over those of the continent, as the result of their individual intelligence; arising in a great degree from the habit of every Frenchman, to discuss whatever topic comes under his notice;

and it is quite unnecessary for me to remark, that the powers of the mind only develop themselves in proportion as they are called into action. Let us hear no more then of soldiers being mere machines. The absurdity of the doctrine is too palpable to need refutation.

   I ought perhaps to assign some reason for having undertaken a labour, to which I may appear so very unequal. It was to relieve my mind from constantly dwelling on a subject of disappointment, which still weighs but too heavily on my spirits; and which I hoped to alleviate, though it cannot be removed by occupation. Personal vanity had no share whatever in it, and if I have not concealed my name, it has been because I hoped to disarm the severity of criticism by avowing it. Much will not be expected from one, who embraced the profession of arms at a very early period, and whose ambition, from a child, has been military and not literary reputation. All that I can flatter myself with having succeeded in, is, the rendering the sense of the author, in terms plain and intelligible. For elegance of style, and flowing periods, the public may look to a Hutchinson, but not to soldiers in general.

John Pine Coffin.

To the Austrian Army
K. Stutterheim

This account of what passed under my own observation at the Battle of Austerlitz, and of the result of my researches on that memorable event, I here dedicate to my brethren in arms. The desire of being read by all the military men in Europe has induced me to write in a language more generally known than that of Germany, and which there are few among you who do not understand. Those who, like myself have borne a part in this disastrous day of the 2nd December, will be enabled to bear testimony to the truth of this narration. I have prided myself on using the greatest impartiality; on having stifled all prepossession, all passion, and every feeling, that could tend to lead my judgment astray. It is to your approbation, my brother soldiers, that I look forward, as the most delightful recompense of all my labours.

Introduction

The imperfect accounts which have reached the public, as to the details of the Battle of Austerlitz, are so contradictory to each other, and so little satisfactory to military men, that it has been thought proper to lay the following relation before them, in order to fix their ideas as to this memorable epoch.

In all ages, as in all countries, nations and armies have been the slaves of opinion. Hence it has ever been the policy of governments to heighten, by those means best calculated to excite national enthusiasm, the splendour of even the greatest victories; as well as to give a specious colouring to those reverses of fortune, which too public to be passed over in silence.

The soldier, who here gives the relation of what he himself saw, neither wishes to flatter a government, nor to gain the good opinion of an army. His object will be, to detail, with truth, what he has either seen or been able to discover from others; and, forgetting the part he himself acted, he will speak with candour and impartiality of the events that passed under his own observation, without the slightest tincture of prejudice, or passion. Of these events, posterity must be the judge.

Nothing will be found here, but the simple recital, without commentary, naked, and devoid of art, of one of the most famous epochs of history. To attempt to reason on the operations of wars that have passed in our times would be giving too much scope to self-love, which always adopts or rejects, as suits our own opinions.

It is not the strength of the respective armies opposed to

each other at the Battle of Austerlitz, or the losses they sustained, which particularly distinguishes it, from many of those which took place in the first campaigns of the French Revolution, and the seven years' war.

We have heretofore often seen 150,000 men in the field, and 30,000 slain. But it is the consequences of the action of the 2nd of December, 1805; it is the epoch when it decided the fate of war; it is the *moment* in which it was fought, which makes it worthy of attention, and which will assign it a marked place in history.

It was the wish to gain personal information that induced the author to collect materials, which may become useful to a better pen: and he avails himself of a leisure moment to offer them to such as have the talent to make use of them.

In order that the past may serve to elucidate the future, it becomes requisite to recur to the circumstances that led to this decisive day; which proved how scrupulously accurate it is necessary to be, in making the calculations and combinations, to which the existing circumstances and the knowledge of human nature give rise.

The Battles of Crems, and of HollaBrünn, are already well known. This is not intended as a history of the late campaign, but merely of a part of it, into which the account of those two affairs does not enter. It was after they had taken place, that M. de Koutousoff directed his retreat upon Brünn, and effected it from that moment, without much annoyance from the enemy. This first Russian Army had orders carefully to avoid a serious engagement, and to hasten its retreat, for the purpose of forming a junction with that under M. de Buxhoevden, who was advancing rapidly to its support. M. de Koutousoff executed a difficult retreat from the River Inn, upon Moravia, which commenced on the 14th October, and lasted till the 18th November; and, although very inferior to the enemy in point of numbers, this Russian Army effected its junction without much loss.

The farther the Grand French Army advanced, the more its combinations became multiplied, and the more it was obliged to detach its force. The Russian general had the advantage of being enabled to concentrate during his retreat, which he also effected in good order: for this he was principally indebted to Prince Bagration, who conducted the rear-guard with much courage.

The two Russian Armies formed their junction at Wischau, on the 18th of November; from which time they became *one*, under the command of the General in Chief, Koutousoff. Its strength consisted of 104 Battalions, 20 of which were Austrians; and 159 squadrons, 54 of which were Austrians, and 40 Cossacks.

The Austrian corps was commanded by Lieutenant General Prince John de Liechtenstein: his infantry was composed of the 6th Battalion, recruited, armed, and organised about a month before; M. de Kienmayer, with the remains of his corps, (very much weakened by the movement of M. de Merveldt on Styria,) formed a part of the corps under Prince John de Liechtenstein. The Archduke Ferdinand, with the wreck of the army from Ulm, and some battalions, also newly raised, was in Bohemia, and thereby covered the right of the combined army; which might at this time be computed at about 72,000 men. The corps under the Archduke Ferdinand was composed of from 18,000 to 20,000 men.

The Grand French Army, after passing the Danube, had advanced into Moravia, being composed of the corps under Prince Murat, Marshals Soult, Lannes, and Bernadotte. The last of these was then opposed to the Archduke Ferdinand, and was advancing upon Iglau. Marshal Davoust, after having followed M. de Merveldt into Styria, moved from Vienna upon Presbourgh. The corps of Marmont marched upon Carinthia, and then upon Styria; in the first instance, to open the communication between the Grand Army and that of Italy; and afterwards, to oppose the junction of the Archduke Charles with the army under M. de Koutousoff; but the movements of this prince were so well calculated, and his force so well concentrated, that he did not allow time for the French to establish themselves at Gratz. Marshal Ney, after the passage of the Inn, took his direction on the Tyrol, by Scharnitz.

At the time of the junction of the two Russian Armies near Wischau, they had only opposed to them, the corps of Prince Murat, part of which formed the advanced guard, those of Marshals Soult and Lannes, the Imperial Guards, under Marshal Bessières, and a corps of grenadiers, drawn from these different troops, forming a reserve of 15,000 men, under General Duroc. This army, when near Brünn, was composed of eight divisions, each of which was about 7,000 strong. The Russian Army was so much fatigued with the continual marches it had been making, whether to fall back on the support, or the support to get forward in time, that it was decided at Wischau to take up the position of Olmutz, to give some days rest to the troops.

Opinions were at that time much divided. The Russian advanced posts had no sort of information as to the position and force of the enemy; at one time, even Prince Bagration was ignorant of the situation occupied by the French advanced guard. The Austrians also, notwithstanding the facility they ought to have possessed of procuring intelligence in the country, had only *very vague data* to act upon.

By this information, however, it appeared, that the French forces were collected only in small numbers near Brünn; and some generals of the combined army gave their opinion at Wischau, for *immediately* resuming the offensive. It is possible, *this moment* might have been more fortunate than that which was afterwards chosen. The strength of the coalesced army was, from the 19th of November, superior to that of the enemy, who was yet uninformed that the junction of the two Russian Armies was effected, and therefore could not expect an offensive movement, such as a manoeuvre on either of his flanks would have been.

****

Note by a French officer.—A general, whose movements are not so combined as to enable him to oppose another manoeuvre to that of his enemy, whatever it may be, is a general devoid of talent, and ignorant of the art of war.

If the Russians had assumed the offensive at Wischau, it would have been previous to the arrival of the corps under the Grand

Duke Constantine, which would have weakened their army by 10,000 chosen men. The French Army would not only have had Marshal Bernadotte with them, who was then at Znaim, but also the corps of Marshal Davoust, whose divisions were in echelons, on Nicolsburgh.

In fact, it was natural to suppose the combined army would not abandon the capital of Moravia without a battle. It was well known that Brünn was a fortified town, that there was much artillery, large magazines of powder, and warlike stores of all kinds in it: its possession seemed to merit an action, and it was expected. Although the arrival of General Buxhoevden was not positively known, yet spies had reported it, and all the information received as to the march of that army in Poland, and the two Galicias, rendered it so probable, that all the calculations of the French Army were founded on the supposition of this junction.

The 19th November, Prince Charles had not passed Goritz; he therefore could not enter into the most remote calculation relative to the war in Moravia. The whole French Army was collected, so that, if the Russian Army had wished to maintain the important point of Brünn, and to defend the magazines in that place, it would two days after have been attacked by Prince Murat, by the corps of Marshals Soult, Lannes, and Davoust, and by part of that under Marshal Mortier. The Russians would have had 10,000 chosen men less than at Austerlitz, and the French 30,000 men more: and if it is asked, why, at Austerlitz, the French had not these 30,000 men more, it is, because the Emperor Napoleon, being informed that the Russian Army was retiring from Wischau, and falling back on Olmutz, conjectured that the Russians were waiting for the third army under Michelson, in order to resume the offensive; or meant to take up a position under the guns of Olmutz, and so wait till Prince Charles approached nearer to the theatre of operation.

Obliged to oppose both these armies; the emperor had detached Marshal Davoust to Presbourgh, and Marshal Ney into Carinthia. The corps under these two marshals would have supported General Marmont, and have had the corps of Marshal Mortier as their reserve; and above 90,000 men would have attacked Prince Charles, before he could approach the Danube:

and, *vice versa*, if the third Russian Army, under Michelson, and the combined army, under Olmutz, (which were calculated by their junction to amount to 120,000 men) should resume the offensive; whether they advanced by Kremsir, or direct upon Brünn, the calculation had been made so as to be joined in a short time, by Marshal Bernadotte, who had made two days march upon Iglau; by Marshal Davoust, one of whose divisions was only two, and the other four marches distant; and lastly, by Marshal Mortier, who would also have arrived in four marches, and who, under this supposition, would have been replaced at Vienna by one of the generals, Marmont or Ney.

These were skilful dispositions; the object of which was, to oppose equal force to the enemy, although in reality superior in numbers to the French Army.

When the Russians assumed the offensive, it was known that Michelson had not joined them. The Emperor Napoleon was of course astonished, and immediately saw how ill combined was the system of the Allies. It was not till after the Battle of Austerlitz, and by reports from Galicia, that it became known that Michelson had no army; that he was only the Inspector of the two other corps; and that the Russians, after the arrival of the Grand Duke Constantine, had nothing more to receive.

As soon as he learnt the offensive movement of the Russians, the emperor recalled Marshal Bernadotte, the remainder of the corps of Marshal Davoust and General Marmont. If he gave battle at Austerlitz, without having been rejoined by the last divisions of Marshal Davoust, and those of Marshal Mortier, it was because he saw so favourable an opportunity, that he not only was persuaded he should gain the battle without these reinforcements, but even had he 30,000 men less.

The Allies then did well to wait the arrival of their reinforcements before they resumed the offensive. They calculated rightly, in letting the emperor be the first to make his movements, and must have conceived the hope of afterwards gaining by it, when they should themselves come to act upon their own plans.

★★★★★★★★★★

The army was then too near him to admit of his receiving reinforcements near Brünn. But this very diversity of opinion, perhaps rendered the movement on Olmutz necessary, because those in command did not possess that decision, which can only be the result of a military eye.

The Austrian general, Weyrother, had been sent into Galicia, for the purpose of conducting the Army of Buxhoevden through the hereditary states. He was an officer of reputation, who did not want for talent, and who had inspired the Russians with confidence. As soon as the two armies became united, he filled the situation of quartermaster general. The court of Vienna had previously selected General Schmidt for this important trust; but that officer, a man of superior merit, and who, with a talent for the profoundest calculation, possessed that tranquil wisdom, which gives reason and deliberation in counsel; after having shewn himself, at Crems, to be worthy of the confidence that was placed in him, lost his life there, and was thus snatched from the hopes of his sovereign, and of his brother soldiers. His loss was the more sensibly felt, and the more regretted, because his successor, neither possessed his calmness, his prudence, or his firmness. The army marched, the 21st of November, from Wischau, and arrived the next day but one, in the position in front of Olmutz, whither we will follow it, for the purpose of detailing the operations.

March of the Combined Army into the Position of Olmutz

It was on the 23rd of November, the army arrived in this position, and was posted in rear of the village of Ollschan. Its left rested on the River March; its right extended to the heights in rear of Tobolau. In this manner it lay upon its arms, in three lines; while the Austrian corps, under Prince John de Liechtenstein, formed the reserve of the army, on the heights in rear of Schnabelin, and was principally intended to secure, in case of a check, the passage across the March. With this view, several bridges were constructed across that river, between Nimlau and Olmutz, to facilitate the operation. The ground occupied by the army in this position, offered great advantages.

It was so commanding, throughout its whole extent, from the heights near Nimlau, to the right of the position, as to discover nearly a league in its front, all the enemy's movements in case of attack; while the slope of the hills in its immediate front was so gentle, as to resemble a glacis. In its rear, spacious ravines, only of sufficient depth to conceal large columns of troops from the enemy, which might unexpectedly be brought into action, facilitated the means, in this *defensive* position, of manoeuvring *offensively*, under cover of the heights. Along their summit, there were commanding points, which mutually defended each other: and on which, the numerous artillery, with which this army was provided, might be employed with great success.

A morass covered the right, and a part of the centre; the Blata ran at the foot of these heights, on which heavy batteries might have been constructed: this little stream, although insignificant in itself, became an additional obstacle, under the fire of grape. To sum up all, the ground offered the means of delaying the enemy, in his attempt to overcome these obstacles, and to open out. The General Bagration, with his advanced guard, was at Prosnitz. General Kienmayer, with his, upon the left, at Kralitz, pushed on detachments upon Klenowitz. The outposts were at Predlitz. An Austrian partisan was sent along the March, on Tobitschau, Kogetein, and Kremsir, to observe that country. The French Army had also sent a partisan, from Goeding on Hradisch, and Kremsir; but the latter was repulsed, and the Austrian detachments remained masters of the March.

It will not escape the observation of intelligent military men, that this was an advantage which gave the Allies the means of manoeuvring by their left, while their right (which would then have rested on the March) was secured; and would have masked this movement, so as to give them, at least two days march in advance. The good understanding, at that time subsisting with Prussia, appears to have been such, as to have made it expedient for the Allied Army, to think of establishing a communication with the Archduke Charles. But, in determining on offensive movements, nothing appears to have been thought of, but going straight forward.

M. de Koutousoff had also sent some Austrian partisans, on his right flank, who marched upon Tribau and Zwittau, whither the Archduke Ferdinand, who was at Czaslau, had sent some parties of light troops, to keep up the chain of communication.

Prince Murat arrived, on the 18th of November, at Brünn. His advanced guard, under General Sebastiani, pushed forward in the first instance, to Rausnitz, and afterwards entered Wischau, after Prince Bagration had evacuated it. The Emperor Napoleon, established himself, on the 20th November, at Brünn, and placed his army in concentrated cantonments, in the following manner:

The corps of guards, the grenadiers of the reserve, and the troops under Marshal Lannes, in Brünn and its vicinity. The cavalry under Prince Murat, on the right and left of the great road, between Brünn and Posorsitz. Marshal Soult, at Austerlitz; and the three divisions, of which his army was composed, were divided, between that place, Butschowitz, Neuwieslitz, Stanitz, and the road to Hungary. At Gaja, was a strong detachment, which kept open the communication with that which observed the River March, in order to secure the right of the army.

****

Note by a French officer.—This disposition, of which the Austrian officer makes mention, and which is accurate, shews that the emperor had foreseen, that the enemy might manoeuvre on the line of operation from Olmutz, along the March; in this case, the Russian Army must pass at Shadish, whence it was farther distant than Marshal Soult, who had some infantry at Gaja, and detachments of cavalry, observing all the route, necessary to this movement.

Whenever the enemy's movement had been known, they would have been allowed to advance. The corps of Marshals Mortier and Davoust, would have been at Goeding, and the enemy would have had 30,000 men to contend with more than at Austerlitz.

In all the enemy's manoeuvres upon Vienna, he moved upon the wings of the French Army, which, by calling in all its detachments, concentrated itself, and opposed its whole force to that of the enemy.

It is more particularly in discussing, what it was possible for the enemy to have done, that we are convinced of the science, and deep calculation shewn by the emperor, in a country so new, and so little known. We see that all his dispositions, even those which appeared to be the most trivial, and to have had no other object in view than the subsistence of the troops, were the result of premeditated design, the chances of which had been already calculated.

****

The 25th November, the Grand Duke Constantine arrived at Olmutz, with the corps of guards, of which he had the command. After a long and forced march from St. Petersburgh, this fine body of men was in the best order.

This corps was composed of ten battalions, and eighteen

squadrons, the whole amounting to 10,000 men; of whom, however, there were only 8,500 under arms. At this moment, the army, under M. de Koutousoff may be computed to have amounted, in all, to above 80,000 men, as will be seen hereafter, in detail.

A reinforcement of 10,000 men was still expected, under General Essen; which, accordingly, arrived near Olmutz, at the moment when the Allied Army commenced its offensive operations. The Corps of Essen was at Kremsir, the day of the battle of Austerlitz, and was of no kind of use. The army under M. de Koutousoff, was certainly stronger than the one opposed to it; but while the *latter* was concentrated towards a single point, and formed into masses, the *former* diffused its force as it advanced. It is not in numbers that the only, and, indeed, the *principal* strength of an army consists; but there are emergencies, and occasions, in which it is absolutely necessary to profit by that advantage; and the present was an instance of the kind. The Allied Army was under the necessity of advancing, for the reasons hereafter to be detailed.

Had it commenced its movement from the day when the Grand Duke Constantine arrived with his reinforcement, forming the reserve of the centre. If, at this epoch, it had manoeuvred with rapidity, and calculation; if the reserve, under the grand duke, had been augmented by the corps under General Essen; if less importance had been attached to the resting an army, which, after some days inactivity, could no longer be fatigued; there might, perhaps, have been found means, without risking a battle, to oblige the French to abandon their position, by turning one of its flanks; which, by giving this army some uneasiness, as to its communications, would have induced it to move upon Vienna, or Bohemia.

The former step would have been attended with danger. The Corps of Bernadotte, which came from Iglau to reinforce the army in front of Brünn, the evening before the Battle of Austerlitz, would not then have had time to make this movement, which was followed by such fatal consequences to the Allies.

(*Note by a French. Officer.*—There is here the mistake of a day. Marshal Bernadotte arrived *two* days before the Battle of Austerlitz.) It was only by means such as these, had the Allies acted with prudence and vigour, that they could have hoped to make the French fall into their combinations: combinations which should have been calmly conceived, and vigorously executed. But the quartermaster general, it has before been mentioned, though an officer of great personal courage, had not that confidence in himself which could enable him to give advice at the headquarters, where the greatest degree of wisdom was requisite. Without regarding the difficulties thrown in his way, this officer, too easily, abandoned his own opinions, to adopt those of other people.

The astonishing rapidity with which the unfortunate events, of this disastrous war, succeeded each other; the excessive folly of Mack, which was only to be surpassed by his disgrace; and in which originated that succession of guilty errors, which astonished Europe, and calumniated a brave army; that folly of never anticipating a check, and of not establishing magazines in the rear, as a consequence of that presumption. To these circumstances it was owing, that the army, while in the position of Olmutz, was almost destitute of provisions.

It had only been there one day, before it was obliged to have recourse to forced requisitions; a violent expedient, which, by the disorderly manner in which it was executed, had much influence on the discipline of the army, into which a spirit of licentiousness began to insinuate itself from that day forwards. In the then state of politics, the gaining time was, at that moment, nearly of equal importance with the gaining a battle: and, the instant it was decided, not to manoeuvre, it became of the highest importance to be enabled to subsist in the position of Olmutz, for the purpose of maintaining it. There still remained countries, from whence it would have been possible to draw provisions; but they were at a distance, and the convoys were obliged to make a long circuit.

To this it was necessary to apply a speedy remedy. The officers of the commissariat received orders, incessantly repeated, but never sufficiently urgent, to establish convoys of provisions, with all possible dispatch, upon the different roads; but *some* of this department wanted both activity and inclination; their systematic conception of things not allowing them to feel the extent of the emergency; while *others* experienced great embarrassment, from the detention, by the Russians, of a great part of the horses belonging to the country, which were employed in the transport of provisions, and were, in consequence, at a loss for the means of conveyance. The bread was plundered on the road, both by the detachments appointed for its escort, and by a number of marauders who followed the army.

The strict discipline, that ought to have existed, was not vigorously maintained, under the pretext, that the army was starving. Relaxation of discipline is always succeeded by excesses; and the licentiousness, attendant upon it, gives full latitude to the disaffected, and to all those who have not courage to support the numerous privations attendant upon modern warfare. It was thought impossible to subsist the army in the position in front of Olmutz, and it was resolved to abandon it, for the purpose of attacking the enemy.

Offensive Movements of the Allied Army

We have already seen the uncertainty in which M. de Koutousoff found himself, as to the movements and force of the enemy, at the moment when it was decided to resume the offensive. The accounts derived from the people of the country were contradictory; and the out-posts gave no information whatever. The first disposition made for the advance, was not then founded upon an exact knowledge both of the position of the enemy and the numbers to be contended with, but was solely adapted to the nature of the ground, between Olmutz and Wischau. This disposition was given to the generals, the 24th November. The 25th was the day on which it was fixed to march; but it was necessary to take two days provisions; and these provisions could not arrive till the day after.

When *that* day came, some of the generals had not sufficiently studied their dispositions; and thus, another day was lost. The enemy profited by this time. The evening before the battle, as has been already mentioned. Marshal Bernadotte, as well as part of the corps of Marshal Davoust, reinforced the Emperor Napoleon. It was necessary to recall the attention to these facts, on which we shall yet have occasion still further to remark.

The 27th November, at eight o'clock in the morning, the army was put in motion, in five columns, to approach nearer the advanced guard, under Prince Bagration, who, on that day, made no movement whatever, in order that the manoeuvre might be concealed from the enemy. This was done with a view to concentrating the troops, which, however, in the, end, were diffused afresh. The five roads, by which the army advanced, were parallel to each other. The two right columns marched along the foot of the mountains, to the right of the causeway, and were composed of infantry only. That of the centre was on the great road to Prosnitz; the fourth to the left of this, and very little distant from it; the fifth, composed entirely of cavalry, was in sight of the fourth. In front of this last, the country was entirely open.

Here follows the detail of the march:

RIGHT WING.

The General of Infantry, Buxhoevden.

First Column.

Lieutenant General Wimpfen.
Major Generals Muller, Sclichow, and Strick.
18 battalions of Russians. 1 company of pioneers.
2½ squadrons of Cossacks.
8,320 men. 250 horses.

Second Column.

Lieutenant General Langeron.
Major Generals Kaminsky, Alsufieu.
18 battalions of Russians. 1 company of pioneers.
2½ squadrons of Cossacks.
11,420 men. 250 horses.

Centre.

The General in Chief, Koutousoff.
Third Column.
Lieutenant General Przybyszewsky.
Major Generals Orosow, Lieders, Lewis,
24 battalions of Russians.
2 companies of reserve artillery.
13,800 men.

LEFT WING.

The Austrian Lieutenant General Prince John de Liechtenstein.

Fourth Column.

The Austrian Lieutenant General Kollowrath.

The Russian Lieutenant Generals Essen and Miloradowich.
The Russian Major Generals Szepelovv and Repninsky.
The Austrian Major Generals Carneville, Rottermunde, and Jurezeck.
32 battalions, of which 20 were Austrians.
1 company of reserve artillery.
5 companies of pioneers.
30 squadrons of Russians, of which 8 were Cosacks.
22,400 men. 3,000 horses.

Fifth Column.

The Austrian Lieutenant General Prince Hohenlohe.
The Russian Lieutenant General Ouwarow.
The Austrian Major Generals Stutterheim, Weber, and Caramelli.
The Russian Major General Piritzky.
70 squadrons, of which 40 were Austrian, but very weak.
2 companies of light artillery,
4,600 horses.

The Reserve.

The Grand Duke Constantine.
Lieutenant Generals Kollagriwoff and Malutin.
Major Generals Jankewitz and Depleradowich.
10 battalions of guards, 4 companies.
18 squadrons.
8,500 men.

RECAPITULATION.

1st and 2nd columns,	36 bat.	2 comp.	5 squad.		19,740
3d do.	24	2			13,800
4th and 5th do.	32	8	100		27,000
Reserve	10	4	18		8,500
Advanced corps under Prince Bagration	12		40*		12,000

General Kienmayer ——- ——— 14 ——- 1,000

114 —- 16 ——- 177 ——† 82,040

* 15 of these were Cosacks.

† *Note by a French officer.*—It is evident that the author here diminishes the real strength of the combined army, by one-*fifth*.

The first column assembled at Nebotin, and marched upon Trzebschein, Blumenau, and Kobelnizeck, where it formed in two lines.

The second column assembled at Olschan, and marched upon Studnitz, Czechowitz, and Ottaslowitz, where it formed, with its right supported by the left of the first column.

The third column assembled on the high road to Prosnitz, on which it marched, and formed in line with the two right columns.

The fourth column assembled at Nedwriss, and marched upon Wrahowitz, and Dobrochow, where it formed, and established its communication with the centre column.

★★★★★★★★★★

Note by the Austrian general.—The Austrian battalions, of which this column was partly composed, were extremely weak, in consequence of the new formation introduced by M. Mack, who, from three battalions to each regiment, made five: and, as before stated, they were new levies, with the exception of the regiment of Salzbourg, and the frontier troops. This corps of infantry was composed as follows:

13

2 bat.	1st reg. of Szeckler.	1 bat. reg. of Lindenau.
2 do.	2d do.	1 ————- Kerpen.
1 do.	Brooder	1 ————- Beaulieu.
6 do.	Salzbourg.	1 ————- Wurtembourg.
1 do.	Auersperg.	1 ————- Reuss. Graitz.
1 do.	Kaunitz.	1 ————- Czartorisky.
		1 ————- Kaiser.
13		20

****

The fifth column assembled at Schabelin, and marched upon Kralitz, and Brzesowitz, where it formed in two lines.

This last column, not being covered by the outposts on the left, had an advanced guard of its own, commanded by General Stutterheim, which communicated with the detachments observing the River March.

The army advanced with much precaution, because it was ignorant of the enemy's movements. It had orders to refuse the left, and to allow the right, which moved along the mountains, to gain ground, in order to turn the enemy's left, in case of meeting with it. The corps under the grand duke marched upon Prosnitz, (where the two emperors and the headquarters were established) and formed the reserve. After four hours march, the army arrived on its different points of formation without any obstacle.

Information was received that the enemy had made no movement whatever, and that his advanced guard at Wischau had neither been reinforced or diminished. Preparations were in consequence made for its attack the next morning, and Prince Bagration received orders to put it in execution. The army was to follow, in the same order as before, the route that should be opened for it by this general.

On the 28th, at daybreak, Prince Bagration put his corps in motion, in three columns; that of the centre remained on the causeway; the two others, on the right and left, turned the town of Wischau; in which the enemy had a regiment of hussars, and one of *chasseurs*. Two other regiments of cavalry were posted in reserve, in rear of the town; while General Sebastiani was at Huluboschan with a regiment of dragoons. As soon as the Russians, with the cavalry under General Kienmayer (composed of the hussars of Szechler and Hesse Hombourg) on their left, appeared before Wischau, and on the heights of Brindlitz, the French cavalry, with the exception of about 100 men, precipitately abandoned the town.

The Adjutant General Dolgorucky, took possession of the

town with two battalions of infantry, and made four officers and 100 men prisoners. The enemy's cavalry received considerable reinforcements in retiring upon Rausnitz, where was a strong reserve. In the first instance, they were pursued by four squadrons of Russian Hussars, and two of Cosacks; but afterwards all the cavalry under Prince Bagration, reinforced by that of the fourth column, under the *command* of Lieutenant General Essen, (under whose orders were placed ten squadrons of *Hulans*, five of *cuirassiers*, five of dragoons, and eight of Cossacks) passed through Wischau, to support the attack of the advanced guard.

To cover his right during this movement, Prince Bagration had received orders to send a regiment of *chasseurs*, and one of cavalry, to the right of Drissitz by Bustomirz and Dietitz, upon Habrowan. This general prosecuted his march as far as the heights of Rausnitz, where he took up his position. The enemy was still master of this little town, and began to cannonade; but the Russian artillery, which was more numerous, soon silenced the fire. In the evening, two Russian battalions took possession of Rausnitz, in front of which were placed the outposts.

M. de Kienmayer, who, with his cavalry, had supported the Russian advanced guard on the left, took his direction upon Drasowitz, and there established his communication with Prince Bagration.

The army, on the 28th, moved, as before, in five columns, and followed up the movement of the advanced guard, in the following manner:

The first column, from Kobelnizech, by Ratzlawitz, upon Lutsch, where it took up its position, posting six battalions of infantry and *chasseurs*, in the wood between Nemajam and Pistomirtz.

The second column, from Ottaslowitz, by Dietitz, upon Nosalowitz, where it formed in second line.

The third column, marched as before, along the causeway, to beyond Noska: one brigade was posted in the first, and the two others in second line.

The fourth column, from Dobrochow, by Krziczanowitz,

and Brindlitz, upon the heights of Noska, where two regiments formed in first line; and the two others in second line. (I am inclined to think the word, *regiment* has here been, inadvertently, substituted for *brigade*. Translator.) The Austrian infantry attached to this column was formed in two lines, on the left of the Russians.

The fifth column, from Brzesowitz, by Ewanowitz, upon Topolan: its advanced guard marched upon Kutscherau, and communicated with that at Drasowitz.

Upon these movements of the Allies, the French quitted their cantonments. By a signal made from Austerlitz, Marshal Soult collected his corps there, which evacuated the villages it had before occupied.

The Allies flattered themselves that the enemy would not risk the fate of a battle in front of Brünn. After the 28th, this *hope* became the prevailing *opinion* at headquarters. Then, instead of hastening their movements, they wished to manoeuvre, at a period, when too much had been risked, to enable them to avoid a decisive action; if, contrary to the opinion of those who thought the French would not fight, they still persisted in not retiring.

We have, hitherto, seen M. de Koutousoff advancing his right, and refusing his left, with the view of turning the enemy's flank by the mountains; for which purpose he had disposed the greater part of his infantry on the right wing. At Wischau this disposition was changed. He wished to manoeuvre on the right of the enemy. A march to the left was undertaken, which both lost time, and the ground that might have been gained to the front. The 29th November, the combined army moved from Lultsch, and the heights of Noska, upon those of Huluboschan and Kutscherau.

It was not till the 1st December that Marshals Bernadette and Davoust joined the Emperor Napoleon and, on the 29th, M. de Koutousoff might have been at Austerlitz. After having passed Wischau, the Allied Army could no longer manoeuvre with impunity. The time it then lost, in making movements, which did not lead it directly towards the enemy, while it discovered its

French Cuirassiers

intentions to the French Army, gave it also the means of receiving such reinforcements as were within reach. A *short* flank movement could not answer the end proposed; while one that was *longer*, would have afforded the enemy an opportunity of attacking on the march.

While the army was moving on the heights of Kutscherau, Prince Bagration pushed on his advanced posts towards Posorsitz: General Kienmayer marched upon Austerlitz, which the enemy had evacuated at ten o'clock, on the morning of the 29th; and General Stutterheim arrived at Butschowitz, from whence he kept up the communication by Stanitz, with a detachment under Lieutenant Colonel Scheither, who had driven the enemy's detachments front Gaja.

★★★★★★★★★★

Note by a French officer.—The corps under Marshal Soult had evacuated Austerlitz at three o'clock in the morning; and was posted at seven o'clock in rear of Puntowitz and Schlapanitz. There are some inaccuracies in the detail of the movements, and the partial attacks; but the narrative is generally correct, and well, told.

★★★★★★★★★★

The French Army concentrated its forces, the same day, between Turas and Brünn: it occupied the villages of Menitz, Tellnitz, Sokolnitz, Kobelnitz, and Schlapanitz, which covered its front, and placed its outposts at Aujest, on the heights of Girshikowitz, and near Krug. The 30th November, the combined army, in consequence of its new plan, again marched to its left, in the following manner:

The first column, from Kutscherau, by Lettonitz, upon Niemschan, which was the appuy for the right; its left was at Hodiegitz, and it was disposed in two lines.

The second column, by Lettonitz, to Hodiegitz, where it formed on the left of the first column.

The third column, upon Malkowitz, by Butschowitz, and Krzisanowitz, where it was posted in reserve, in rear of the first column.

The fourth column, by Schardiska, Tschertschein, Krzizanowitz, upon Herspitz, where it formed in reserve to the second column.

The fifth column, by Neuwieslitz, followed the march of the third, and was posted in the valley, in front of Marhoefen.

The Reserve, under the Archduke Constantine, marched to Butschowitz; the advanced corps, under Prince Bagration, to Posorsitz; and pushed on its outposts upon the causeway, and upon Krug. M. de Kienmayer remained at Austerlitz, and was reinforced by the brigade under General Stutterheim. A little affair of outposts took place that day; the enemy was employed in reconnoitring, and a few cannon shots were ineffectually exchanged. The headquarters of M. de Koutousoff were at Hodiegitz; those of the two emperors at Krzizanowitz, near Austerlitz.

It is here necessary to remark, that during these offensive movements the Archduke Ferdinand had received orders to advance also, to make a diversion and occupy the enemy; and that this prince, quitting Czaslau, after having driven the Bavarians, first from Steinsdorff and afterwards from Deutschbrod, was advancing upon Iglau, where the Bavarian general, De Wrede, had the command.

On the 1st December, there was a good deal of firing, the whole of the morning, along the entire chain of out-posts. The enemy, from day-break in the morning, was continually reconnoitring along the heights in front of Pratzen and Krug. He also, for the like purpose, pushed parties from his left to beyond the high road. M. de Kienmayer's outposts, on the left, were at Satchan: and he had a post near Menitz, a village which the French abandoned. Five battalions of frontier troops, under Major-General Carneville, being a part of the Austrian infantry, arrived in the evening to reinforce M. de Kienmayer.

The combined army, the left of which was commanded by General Buxhoevden, and the centre by the general-in-chief, after having dined, moved forwards, in five columns, in the following manner:

The first column, under Lieutenant-General Dochtorow,

composed of twenty-four battalions of Russians, marched by its left on Herspitz, Wachan, Klein-Hostieradeck, and took up a position in two lines, on the heights where this village is situated. A regiment of *chasseurs* was posted at Aujest, a village between the foot of the mountain and the lakes of Menitz.

The second column, commanded by Lieutenant-General Langeron, composed of eighteen battalions of Russians, marched by Austerlitz, Krzenowitz, and took up a position on the heights of Pratzen; also, in two lines on the right of the first column.

The third column, commanded by Lieutenant-General Przybyszewsky, composed of eighteen battalions of Russians, marched on the right of Austerlitz, took its direction upon Pratzen, and its position on the heights, to the right of this village.

The fourth column, commanded by the Austrian Lieutenant-General Kollovvrath, was composed of twelve battalions of Russians, under Lieutenant-General Miloradowitsch, and of fifteen of Austrians, who were in the rear of this column. This latter marched by its right, near Niemschan, intersected the high road from Austerlitz to Brünn, and took post in two lines, in rear of the third column.

The fifth column, composed of cavalry, under the orders of Lieutenant-General Prince John, of Liechtenstein, was composed of eighty-two squadrons, marched by its left, and followed the direction of the third column, behind which it took post under the heights.

The corps of reserve, under the Grand Duke Constantine, composed of ten battalions, and eighteen squadrons of guards, passed by Austerlitz, and posted itself on the heights in front, with its left towards Krzenowitz, and its right towards the high road from Austerlitz to Brünn.

The advanced corps, under Prince Bagration, extended by its left beyond Holubitz and Blasowitz, in order to facilitate the inarch of the third and fourth columns upon their points of formation.

Lieutenant-General Kienmayer, as soon as the columns arrived on the heights, in front of Austerlitz and Krzenowitz,

French Infantry of the Line

where his troops were posted, marched by Pratzen, in front of Aujest, where he arrived at nine o'clock at night: his corps was then composed of twenty-two squadrons of Austrians, ten of Cossacks, and five battalions of Croats.

The headquarters were at Krzenowitz. The enemy did not interrupt this movement, and even withdrew his out-posts as far as Tellnitz, Sokolnitz and Schlapanitz. The second column having arrived late on its point of formation, had no outposts in its front. *During the whole night there was no chain of outposts established in front of the position occupied by the combined army.*

At one moment during the night, the enemy evacuated the village of Tellnitz, in which out-posts were placed by a half squadron of Austrian light cavalry of the regiment of O'Reilly: but two hours after, the French returned in force, and posted a regiment of infantry in this village, from the division of Legrand, forming a part of the right of Marshal Soult. The out-posts on the left of the Allies sent, continually, patrols during the night, to their right, in order to establish a communication with the Russian advanced posts, but could never fall in with them.

This offensive movement had been made by the army in open day, and in sight of the enemy, who, from the heights of Schlapanitz, and in front of Kobelnitz, had been able to remark it at his ease. The position occupied by the Allies, at the moment when they crowned the heights between Aujest, Pratzen, and Holubitz, was a strong one: The enemy, had he been well observed, would have found it difficult to advance for the purpose of attacking these heights.

****

Note by a French officer.—There is no foundation for the remark here made by the Austrian officer; since the emperor, who intended to act upon the centre of the enemy, had an interest in remaining master of these defiles, that no obstacle might be opposed to the bringing his army into action: it was with this view he occupied the fine position of the Santon, situated in front of all the small streams: besides, the emperor had posts upon these rivulets two days before; and the left of the French Army was between the Santon and the village of Girshikowitz, which was the rendezvous of almost the whole cavalry; consequently, from that moment, it was no longer necessary to pass the defiles in order to attack the heights.

This observation of the Austrian officer, only serves to mark more strongly to every French officer, who was a witness of the affair, both the prudence and military eye of their general. He made the Santon, the point of appuy, for his left flank; not because it was a fine defensive position; there were others in the rear equally good; but *because it was the key to all offensive operations*. If, on the contrary, the French general had neglected the Santon, the whole of the left wing of the French Army would have been prevented from resuming the offensive, unless they passed the defiles.

Eight days before the battle, the emperor returning from Wischau, ascended the Santon, notwithstanding the extreme cold; and said to the officers about him: "Examine this position well; it will probably play a conspicuous part before two months are over our heads."

The emperor having always had it in view, during the campaign in Moravia, not to allow his left to be turned, and to abandon his right; that alone would have been a sufficient reason for resting his left on a position not defensive, but offensive, such as was that of the Santon. The fact is, the more we discuss the plan of the campaign, the more we perceive the judgment and military eye of a master in the science of war.

****

The defiles of Tellnitz, Sokolnitz, and Schlapanitz, which separated the two armies, offered the means of delay; and the very elevated points of these heights afforded strong means of defence. Here, as in the position, in front of Olmutz, the army was posted on a curtain, behind which massive columns might be posted, ready to act offensively. Its left was secured by the lakes of Menitz and Aujest, while the right was refused. But the taking advantage of this position was never thought of, any more than the possibility of being *attacked* on these heights, or of finding the enemy on this side the defile.

The French emperor took advantage, in a masterly manner, of the faults that were committed. He kept his troops concentrated in massive columns, ready to act according to circumstances. Marshal Bernadotte (who had joined the Emperor Napoleon the day on which the Allies shewed themselves on the heights of Pratzen), had been posted in the first instance to the left of the high road. In the night the emperor caused his corps to pass this road, and posted it in rear of the village of Girschikowitz, which was occupied in force. This corps, composed of the divisions of Rivaux and Drouet, formed the centre of the French Army.

Prince Murat's cavalry was in rear of Marshal Bernadotte, and on his left. Marshal Lannes formed the left wing with the divisions of Suchet and Caffarelli; this last was connected with the left of Prince Murat. The right of the army, commanded by Marshal Soult, was placed between Kobelnitz and Sokolnitz; the division of Legrand forming the extreme right, was posted between Sokolnitz and Tellnitz, and occupied these villages with strong detachments of infantry. The division of Vandamme was on the left, and the division of St. Hilaire in the centre of Marshal Soult's corps.

The reserve of the army, composed of ten battalions of the Imperial Guard, and of ten battalions of General Oudinot's corps, the whole commanded by General Duroc, was near Turas. The division of Friant, belonging to the corps under Marshal Davoust, which had just arrived from Presburg, was sent to the convent of Reygern, on the Schwartza, to observe and keep the enemy in check, should he approach by the route of Auspitz. The division of General Gudin (also arrived from Presburg), with some dragoons belonging to Marshal Davoust's corps, advanced from Nickolsbourg, on the right of the French Army, to keep in check the corps of M. de Merveldt, who had penetrated through Hungary to Lundenebourg.

This general had with him his own regiment of *Hulans*, and the emperor's hussars, much weakened by the losses they had sustained during a difficult retreat; and six battalions of infantry, also very weak; the whole amounting to little more than 4,000 men. A detachment of O'Reilly's light cavalry, and some Cossacks, were sent to Gros-Niemschitz to observe that point.

We have now given the position of both armies, during the night between the 1st and 2nd December, which immediately preceded this ever-memorable day.

Battle of Austerlitz

The disposition for the attack of the French Army was delivered to the general officers of the Austro-Russian Army, soon after midnight, on the morning of the 2nd December. But the imperfect knowledge that was possessed of their position, although scarcely out of range of the enemy's musketry, naturally made the suppositions upon which the disposition of attack was founded also very indefinite. Some movements had been remarked, the evening before, on the enemy's left, but it was not known to be occasioned by the arrival of the corps under Marshal Bernadotte.

★★★★★★★★★★

Note by a French officer,—Marshal Bernadotte was never seen till the day of the battle. *Two* days before he had rested on his arms behind Brünn, and the following day he took post in the rear of the army, near Lattein. The French generals object in this disposition was, not only to avoid fatiguing this corps as much as possible, but also, not to pass the defile of Bellowitz; for not intending to risk an action, unless the enemy committed great errors, he had determined on retiring another day's march to the rear, if the enemy manoeuvred with skill. It was not his wish to engage a general action with a superior army, if it were well posted. The victory might have been doubtful, and above all, too destructive.

It was, therefore, that the divisions repassed the defiles, each day in proportion as the enemy's plans became apparent, and the faults he was about to commit became more probable. Besides, if instead of turning the right of the French Army, (which was what the French general rather wished) the Russians had

Bivouac on the eve of the battle

brought on an affair among the mountains, by turning the left. The position of the headquarters, behind Kritchen, (which was always occupied by the French) was the point, from whence, by a wheel to the left, it was the most easy to move diagonally in rear of the Santon, upon the little hills towards the left.

The movement that may have been seen on our left, was nothing else than the posting the divisions of Suchet and Caffarelli to support the Santon, because it was apprehended the enemy might, in the course of the day, attempt to get possession of that height, which was the key to the emperor's projects. He would not allow the enemy to occupy positions too near to Girshikowitz and Puntowitz, which might have prevented the army from forming. For the attack, which had been planned by the emperor, particularly depended on the rapidity with which the centre should march on the heights of Pratzen.

****

It was supposed that the French Army was weakening its centre to reinforce its left. Several lines of smoke, which had also been perceived the evening before, between Turas and the lakes in rear of Sokolnitz, and Kobelnitz, and some others near Czernowitz, caused the belief that the French Army had made these lakes the point of appuy for their right, and had placed a reserve in the rear. The left of the combined army outflanked the right of the French Army. It was supposed, that by passing the defile of Sokolnitz, and of Kobelnitz, their right would be turned, and that the attack might afterwards be continued in the plain, between Schlapanitz and the wood of Turas, thus avoiding the defiles of Schlapanitz and Bellowitz, which, it was believed, covered the front of the enemy's position.

The French Army was then to be attacked by its right flank, upon which it was intended to move down large bodies of troops; this movement was to be executed with celerity and vigour; the valley between Tellnitz and Sokolnitz was to be passed with rapidity; the right of the Allies (on which was the cavalry of Prince John de Liechtenstein, and the advanced corps under Prince Bagration) was to cover this movement.—The first of these generals on the plain between Krug and Schlapanitz, on each side of the causeway; and the other by protecting the cavalry, and occupying the heights situated between Dwaroschna and the Inn of Lesch, with his artillery.

****

Note by a French officer.—This plan was faulty in every point of view. Supposing the emperor not to have attacked the heights of Pratzen, merely keeping possession of the Santon, and the village of Girshikowitz, he would have made an effort in the centre, when the enemy attacked him, and the left of the enemy, once arrived at the wood of Turas, was by that divided from his centre.

All this serves to prove, that many men are capable of manoeuvring 15,000 or 20,000 men, but very few know how to derive all the possible advantage from an army of 80,000.

****

For this purpose, the five columns, composed as before, received orders to advance in the following manner:

1st. Column. Lieut.-General Dochtorow, with 24 battalions of Russians, from the heights of Hostieradeck, by Aujest, upon Tellnitz. After having passed the village and defile, the column was to move forward to the right upon the lakes, till its head became parallel with that of the 2nd column.

2nd Column. Lieut.-General Langeron, with 18 battalions of Russians, marching like the former column, by his left from the heights of Pratzen, was to force the valley between Sokolnitz and Tellnitz, and then dress by the 1st column.

3rd Column. Lieut.-General Przybyszewsky, with 18 battalions of Russians, was also to move by his left, from the heights to the right of Pratzen, close by the castle of Sokolnitz; from whence the heads of the three columns were to move forward, between Sokolnitz and the lakes situated behind it, as far as the lakes of Kobelnitz.

4th Column. Lieut.-General Kollowrath, with 27 battalions, 15 of which were Austrian, moving forward by his left, from the heights in rear of the 3rd column, was to pass the same valley, and the lakes of Kobelnitz, and bring the head of his column parallel with that of the three former.

The advanced corps under M. Kienmayer, was to protect, with its infantry, the movements of the 1st column, so that this last was, in fact, reinforced by five Austrian battalions, and composed altogether of 29 battalions. The heads of these four columns of infantry were to present a large front, and four battalions of the 1st column were to occupy the wood of Turas. The remainder, and all the other columns, were then to move forward between this wood and Schlapanitz, and to attack the right of the enemy with strong bodies of infantry, while three battalions of the fourth column should be occupied in carrying the village of Schlapanitz.

5th Column. Lieut.-General Prince John de Liechtenstein, with 82 squadrons, was first of all to move from the foot of the hill, in rear of the 3rd column, between Blasowitz and Krug, to protect the formation and march of the columns on the right, and afterwards to advance upon the plain on the right and left of the causeway, between Krug and the Inn of Lesch, as was before mentioned.

The advanced corps, under Lieutenant-General Prince Bagration, consisting of twelve battalions and forty squadrons, was to maintain its position, and gain the heights between Dwaroschna, and the Inn of Lesch, in order to place strong batteries of cannon upon them.

The corps of reserve, under the Grand Duke Constantine, consisting of ten battalions and eighteen squadrons, was to move from the heights in front of Austerlitz to the rear of Blasowitz and Krug; he was to serve as a support to the cavalry of Prince John de Liechtenstein, and to the corps under Prince Bagration.

The fortune of this day was made to depend upon the rapidity of the attack on our left, and on the driving back the enemy's right upon *his* left. It was imagined the battle would not be decisive if Prince Bagration was not enabled to oppose an obstinate resistance to the attacks the French might make upon him; and orders were given to the cavalry, under Prince John de Liechtenstein, to attack the enemy in any movement he might make,

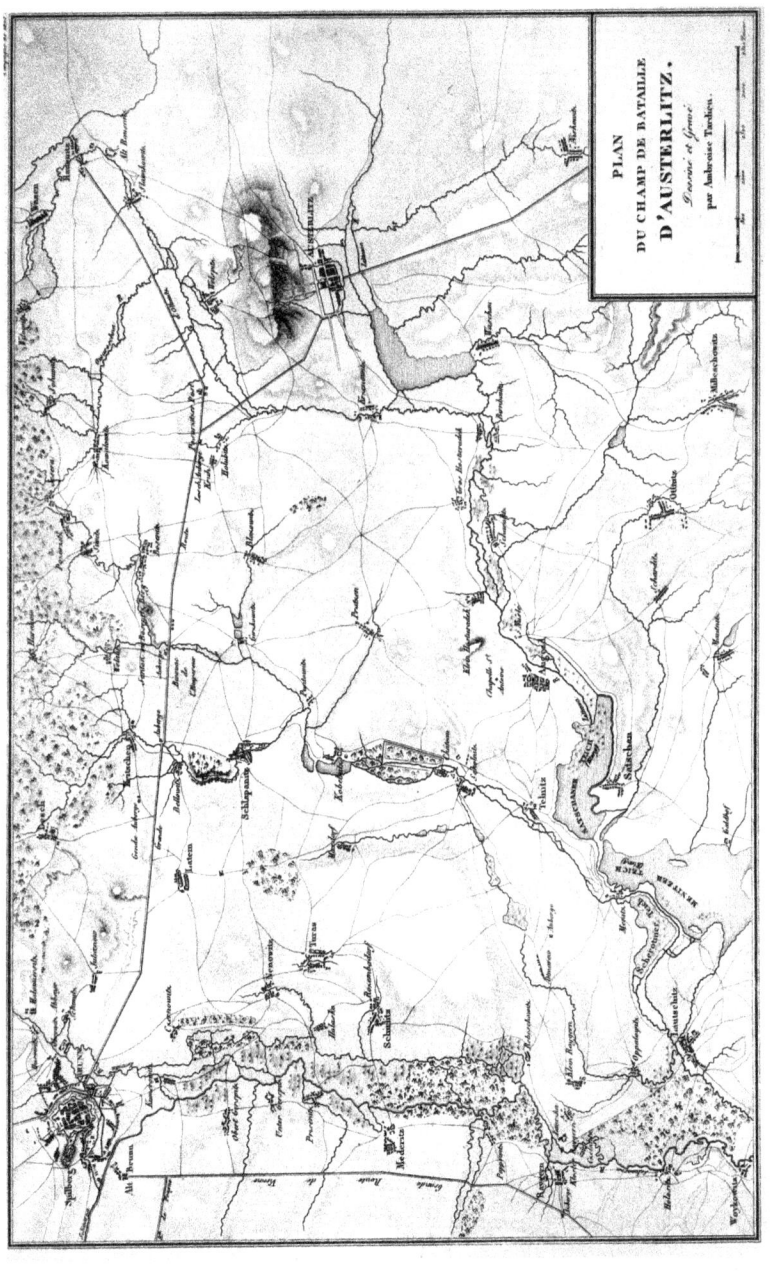

with a view to engaging this Russian general.

The cavalry, under Lieutenant-General Kienmayer, as soon as the first column should have passed the defile of Tellnitz, was destined to cover the left of the column, and to march between Turas and the Schwarza; observing well the convent of Reygern.

It was settled in the disposition, that in case the four columns were fortunate enough to advance as far as the causeway between Lattein and Bellowitz, and to drive the enemy back into the mountains, the Wood of Turas was *still* to remain occupied by the four battalions destined to this purpose, in order to preserve the facility of manoeuvring round it, and the means of retiring, if necessary, by Kobelnitz and Puntowitz into the position of Pratzen; which retreat was, in case of the worst, to be continued as far as the position of Hodiegitz, Niemtschen, and Herspitz.

If the attack made by the left proved successful, then Prince Bagration was to move against the enemy's left, and to establish a communication with the four columns of infantry; after which it was intended to unite the army in front of the village of Lattein, between Lesch and Nennowitz. The defiles of Schalapanitz, Bellowitz and Kritschen, being thus cleared, the cavalry under Prince John de Liechtenstein was to pass them with rapidity, in order to support the infantry; and, in case of success, to pursue the enemy between Brünn and Czernowitz.

The general-in-chief, Koutousoff, was in the centre with the fourth column.

The general of infantry, Buxhoevden, commanded the left of the army, and marched with the first column.

Having thus given the plan of attack, concerted by the Allies, we are now about to see the manner in which it was deranged, and how it happened that the faults in the conception were not compensated for by the success of the execution.

At seven o'clock in the morning the combined army was put in motion, and quitted the heights of Pratzen to advance upon its given points. Each of the four columns of infantry was perfectly in view of the enemy, who could not but perceive that the direction of their march caused considerable intervals between them, in proportion as the heads of the columns approached the valleys of Tellnitz, Sokolnitz and Kobelnitz. The action began on the left wing of the Allies. The corps of General Kienmayer, posted in front of Aujest, as before mentioned, was nearest the enemy, and destined to force the defile of Tellnitz, to open the route for the first column, which had a great circuit to make after having passed this defile, in order to arrive at the point which would bring it in a line with the second column; this made it necessary to carry the village of Tellnitz as soon as possible.

Between Aujest and Tellnitz is a considerable plain, on which some squadrons of hussars were advanced, between seven and eight o'clock, to reconnoitre the enemy. On a hill, in front of the village, were posted several companies of infantry, who defended its approach, while some detachments of cavalry were on the right, having the lake of Menitz as their appuy.

M. de Kienmayer ordered a detachment of cavalry to advance against their right, and a battalion of the first, regiment of Szeckler infantry to attack the hill on which the French infantry was posted.

★★★★★★★★★★

> Many misfortunes of the Allies appear to have originated in attacking with small corps where they had the power of attacking in force. It is obvious, that if one battalion is inadequate to the service on which it is sent, it will not only suffer severely in the attempt, but that very attempt will apprize the enemy of the intention, and enable him to reinforce. Whereas, by at once attacking with numbers, all opposition is borne down, and the defence, from not being protracted, is generally less destructive to the assailants: wherever the French make an attack, it is in force; and *therefore*, they usually succeed; with the additional advantage, that they are enabled *by those very numbers* to maintain themselves in what they have acquired. Translator.

★★★★★★★★★★

The latter was reinforced, and a fire of musketry commenced, which became pretty warn. The French defended themselves with obstinacy; and the Austrians, who had been supported by another battalion, attacked with spirit.

The hussars of Hesse Hombourg, on the right, under Major General Nostitz, and those of Szeckler on the left, under Major General Prince Maurice Liechtenstein, took post on the flanks of this infantry, to check the enemy's cavalry, (which was perceived on the farther side of the defile of Tellnitz) should it attempt to pass for the purpose of attacking these Austrian battalions. The hussars suffered severely from the enemy's sharp shooters, who took advantage of the ground, which all round the village was covered with vineyards, and full of ditches; but they could not succeed in keeping off the cavalry.

The second battalion of the regiment of Szeckler infantry had arrived to reinforce the first, which was attacking the hill, and which had lost more than half its strength. Twice the Austrians were repulsed; and twice they again advanced to the foot of the hill, which it was necessary to carry, in order to arrive at the village. At length General Stutterheim succeeded in getting possession of it with these two battalions.

The enemy's third regiment of the line, and two battalions of sharp shooters, were in possession of Tellnitz and the vineyards round the village. These troops defended their post with valour. M. de Kienmayer ordered General Carneville to advance with the remainder of his infantry (consisting of three other battalions) to the support of the two which were on the hill, and were fighting with great courage.

A destructive fire of musketry ensued, the village was situated in a natural entrenchment, the vineyards being surrounded by a deep ditch, of which the French kept possession: however, the Austrians succeeded at one time in penetrating as far as the village; but were again repulsed, and had some difficulty in maintaining possession of the hill they had before carried.

The regiment of Szeckler infantry fought with the greatest obstinacy; above two-thirds of them being killed or wounded. This action had already lasted above an hour, and yet the head of the first column, with which was M. de Buxhoevden, had not yet made its appearance. The French had more troops belong-

The Battle of Austerlitz

ing to Legrand's division on the farther side of the defile; and the Austrians engaged in so unequal a contest (since they were without support), continued to make fresh efforts, which they momentarily expected would become useless.

At length, M. de Buxhoevden, with the first column, appeared from Aujest, and sent a battalion of the Seventh regiment of Light Infantry to support the Austrians, and a brigade of Russians to form the reserve. Two Austrian battalions, with this battalion of light infantry, which charged the enemy with impetuosity, attacked the village, gained possession of it, and were followed by the remainder. The French, on the approach of such superior numbers, evacuated the defile, and drew up on the farther side in order of battle. M. de Buxhoevden, before he moved forward, waited to see the head of the second column (which was not advancing) appear in the plain, between the foot of the hills and Sokolnitz.

Towards nine o'clock the enemy received a reinforcement of 4,000 men from the corps under General Davoust. These troops arrived from the convent of Reygern; the French then taking advantage of a thick fog which suddenly darkened the whole valley, again got possession of the village, and even penetrated as far as the hill beyond it. At this moment General Nostitz made a rapid charge, with two squadrons of the hussars of Hesse Hombourg, for the purpose of checking them.

The Russian light infantry, and an Austrian battalion, which had been posted in Tellnitz, had fallen back in disorder: the Russian regiment of New Ingermannland ought to have supported them; but retreated in a manner, which, combined with the fog, threw a part of the column into confusion. The charge made by the hussars had checked the French infantry, some hundreds of whom were made prisoners. The fog having dispersed, the troops again moved forwards, and the enemy abandoned the village. The first column made a deployment in several lines upon the hill, and Tellnitz was retaken.

A cannonade took place; and as soon as the French entirely withdrew from this point, the defile was passed, without opposition, by the brigades of cavalry under Prince Maurice Liechtenstein and General Stutterheim, who drew up in order of battle on the farther side. Tellnitz and the defile were occupied by some battalions provided with artillery.

The enemy then entirely abandoned the plain between Tellnitz and Turas; but he was not followed up, because the communication with the second column was not yet established. The Austrian cavalry consequently avoided the snare laid for it, by the retreat of the right of the French Army. During this action, near Tellnitz, the second and third column had quitted the heights of Pratzen, and had approached towards Sokolnitz, which was occupied by two battalions from the division of Legrand. These two battalions opposed some resistance to the Russian light infantry as they advanced at the head of these columns. The French had placed some cannon on a hill between Sokolnitz and Kobelnitz; (the latter village was occupied by the enemy's reserve) a pretty heavy cannonade was opened upon Sokolnitz, which destroyed the village.

These two Russian columns, without concerning themselves as to the fourth column, without any direct communication with it, and without being deterred by the offensive movements of the enemy, thought of nothing but the first disposition, and continued their movements upon Sokolnitz; which village they took possession of without much resistance, after a long and useless cannonade. General Muller, of the Russian light infantry, was wounded and afterwards taken prisoner beyond Sokolnitz. In passing this village, the two columns crossed upon each other, and some confusion ensued.

We must now, for an instant, leave this point, in order to see what was passing in the centre, and on the right of the Allies, while the capture of the villages of Tellnitz and Sokolnitz was going forward. The Emperor of the French, who had not failed to remark the want of concert and consistency in the movements of the Austro-Russian Army, and who saw that by the circuitous route the left was obliged to take, it became more distant from the centre, in proportion as it advanced, immediately put in motion the massive columns which he had kept together, with a view of marching against the centre, and by that means cutting off the wing, which still imprudently continued to advance, for the purpose of turning the French Army in a position which it did not occupy.

The Reserve of the French Army, composed of ten battalions of the Imperial Guard, and of ten battalions of General Oudinot's grenadiers, (who recovered from his wound, now resumed his command) remained upon the heights between Schlapanitz and Kobelnitz. This Reserve did not fire a shot during the whole battle. Marshal Soult, with the two divisions of St. Hilaire, and Vandamme (posted during the night, as we have already seen, in the valley of Kobelnitz), traversed this village and that of Puntowitz, to make an attack upon the heights and the village of Pratzen.

At the same time Marshal Bernadotte, after having crossed, by means of a bad and narrow bridge, (only a few musket shots distant from his enemy) the rivulet at the village of Girschikowitz, with the division of Rivaud on his left, and that of Drouet on his right, took his direction upon the heights of Blasowitz. The cavalry under Prince Murat formed in several lines on the left of Marshal Bernadotte, and marched between Girschikowitz and Krug. Marshal Lannes having on his right the division of Caffarelli, and on his left that of General Suchet, moved forward to the left of Prince Murat, on each side of the causeway. From that time the centre and right of the Allies became engaged in all quarters.

The Grand Duke Constantine was destined with the corps of guards to form the Reserve of the right, and quitted the heights in front of Austerlitz, at the appointed hour, to occupy those of Blasowitz and Krug. He was hardly arrived on this point before he found himself in *first line*, and engaged with the sharp shooters of Rivaud's division, and Prince Murat's light cavalry, commanded by General Kellermann. The grand duke hastened to occupy the village of Blasowitz with the light infantry battalion of the guards. At the same instant Prince John de Liechtenstein arrived with his cavalry.

According to the original disposition, this prince was to post himself on the left of Prince Bagration, to preserve the command of the plain in front of Schlapanitz. This column of cavalry, which had been posted in rear of the third column, and which was to move by its right flank, upon its point of attack, was impeded in its march by the columns of infantry, which crossed upon it as they were advancing, to descend from the heights. Prince Liechtenstein had hastened to send, daring the march, 10 squadrons, under Lieut.-General Uwarrow, to the left of Prince Bagration, to secure that general's left flank, which was opposed to a part of Prince Murat's cavalry.

After the regiment of Elisabethgrod hussars had formed in order of battle, under General Uwarrow, the Grand Duke Constantine's regiment of *Hulans* became the head of the column of cavalry. Prince John de Liechtenstein, when he arrived on the grand duke's left, found the enemy in presence of the Russian guards; it was the cavalry under General Kellermann, supported by the infantry of Marshal Bernadotte's left, and of Marshal Lannes' right. Prince John de Liechtenstein immediately determined on forming his cavalry in order of battle, to charge the enemy. The grand duke's regiment was the first that deployed; but, carried away by the ardour of the brave General Essen, who commanded them; the *Hulans* did not await the formation of the rest of the line, and, without support, rushed forward to attack the enemy's light cavalry, which, retiring through the intervals of the infantry, was pursued with but too much impetuosity through the battalions.

****

> Either there were two generals of this name in the Russian Army, or there must be some mistake; since, in a former part of this work, General Stutterheim says, "The corps under Essen was at Kremsir on the day of the battle, and was of no sort of use."—Translator.

****

The *Hulans* wanted to attack the French cavalry that was in second line, but in consequence of the fire they had sustained, they reached it in disorder, and were received by it with determination. The division of Caffarelli formed a line on their right, and that of Rivaud on their left, and the *Hulans*, being thus placed between two fires, lost above 400 men; Lieut.-general Essen, who led them, was severely wounded, and died in consequence. The grand duke's regiment, which had made this brilliant charge, attacked too soon, with too much impetuosity, and became the victim of its own ill-placed courage. It was put completely to the route, and in this state, it reached, by its right, the corps under Prince Bagration, in rear of which it again formed. This last general had now moved forward from the post of Posorsitz, to oppose the left of Marshal Lannes, which rested on Kovalowitz; Prince Bagration had caused the villages of Krug and Holubitz to be occupied by General Ulanius, with three battalions of light infantry.

We now come to the centre of the Allied Army, where the fate of this day was decided. It was too weak to resist the enemy's attacks. Abandoned by the third column, and all the left of the army, while the division on the right flank was not sufficiently powerful to divide the French forces; the centre saw itself attacked, or menaced with attack, by *four* divisions, to which it could only oppose 27 very weak battalions, without any hope of reinforcement. Those Russian regiments which had made their retreat from Braunau, formed a part of this number, and were scarcely composed of 400 men each.

Without exaggeration, we may here calculate, that 12,000 men were attacked by 24,000, and while the French Army was not, in fact, so numerous as that of the Allies, by a more happy arrangement of their force, which was more concentrated and better directed, the enemy's strength was *doubled* on that point, which was of the greatest importance. The centre of the Allies was perfectly insulated, which, in consequence of the distance the several columns (the 2nd and 3rd excepted) were from each other, was the case, nearly, on *all* points.

The Emperor of Russia, with the commander in chief, arrived at the head of the fourth column, at the moment when it was to advance. In order to give time to the columns on the left to gain ground, Lieut.-General Kollowrath, who commanded the fourth column, received orders not to move till towards eight o'clock. The action, therefore, near Tellnitz, had already begun, and the left was in motion, when the centre formed, and broke into platoons from the left.

The Russian infantry, under Lieut.-General Miloradowich, was at the head of the column. Two of his battalions, of the regiments of Novogrod and Apscherousky, commanded by Lieut.-Colonel Monachtin, with some Austrian dragoons of the Archduke John's regiment, formed the advanced guard of the column, and marched only a small distance in its front.

It was now near nine o'clock, and the third column had just quitted the heights of Pratzen to march, in conformity to the disposition, upon Sokolnitz: the fourth column had just arrived on the ground occupied, during the night, by General Przibischewsky, when a massive column of French infantry was suddenly descried in a bottom, in front of Pratzen. As soon as the enemy's columns were perceived, they were put in motion, at the moment when the Russian advanced guard approached the village. This massive column of the enemy was composed as follows: the right columns of the division of Vandamme; those on the left, of the division of St. Hilaire.

Nevertheless, the advanced guard of the 4th column lost no time in occupying the village of Pratzen, and got possession of a small bridge beyond it before the enemy's sharp shooters. Having passed this bridge, it posted a battalion upon a hill to the left, in front of the village, (which was not yet left by the rear of the third column) while the other battalion of the advanced guard occupied the village itself.

General Koutousoff, whom this movement of the enemy had taken by surprise (thinking himself the assailant, and seeing himself attacked in the midst of his combinations and his movements), felt all the importance of maintaining the heights of Pratzen, against which the French were moving; they commanded everything, and were the only security to the rear of

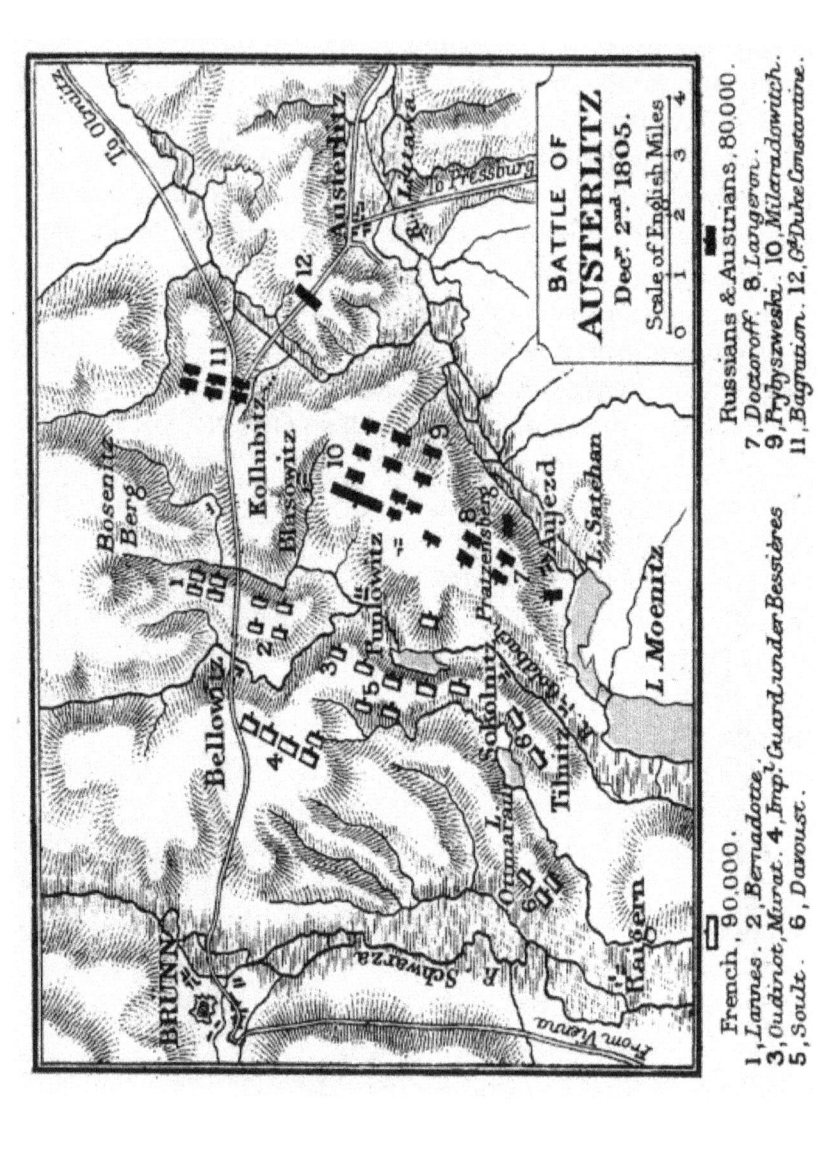

the third column, which continued to advance and expose itself with the greatest imprudence, forgetting the enemy and everything but the original disposition. It was the summit of the heights of Pratzen which decided the fate of the day. It had been the key to the position the Allied Army had just quitted; and, from the confused situation of the different columns their fate depended upon whoever was master of this height.

As soon as the commander-in-chief, who was at the head of the column, was informed by his advanced guard that the enemy was so near him, he gave orders for shewing him a front, and for occupying the height; at the same time, he sent for some cavalry from the column under Prince John de Liechtenstein, who sent him four Russian regiments. The French directed the march of their two masses of infantry with great coolness, and at a slow pace. A third column of the enemy now made its appearance on the right of Pratzen, and threatened to pass through the interval, between the fourth column, and the cavalry under Prince John de Liechtenstein.

This French column was a part of the corps under Marshal Bernadotte. Upon this the Russian infantry, belonging to the fourth column, marched to the right of Pratzen, and sent a reinforcement to the battalions of the advanced guard, which were already posted on the hill to be maintained; but this advanced guard, being attacked by superior numbers, abandoned it, after a very short resistance.

The action then became very warm, and it was attempted to regain the ground that had been lost by the advanced guard. The Russians made an attack; opened their fire at too great a distance, and without much effect, while the French columns continued to advance without firing a shot; but when at the distance of about a hundred paces, they opened a fire of musketry which became general, and very destructive. The enemy opened out his masses by degrees, formed in several lines, and marched rapidly towards the height, resting his left on the church of the village, and his right on the most elevated point of the heights. Having reached them, he formed in an angular direction, for the purpose of opposing the rear of the third column. This was composed of the brigade under General Kamensky, which had separated from the column, and shewed a front upon the height, menacing the right flank of Marshal Soult's corps.

It was still necessary to dislodge the enemy from the heights, of which he had obtained possession, and to prevent his establishing himself on them.

The Emperor of Russia, who, during this sanguinary conflict, had remained with his infantry of the fourth column, and who, incessantly, exposed his own person in trying to remedy the confusion, ordered his battalions to advance, and try to take the enemy in flank. General Kollowrath received orders to check the enemy on the left, and, for that purpose, caused the Austrian brigades, under the Generals Jurczeck and Rottermund, to advance against the heights, on which the French continued to gain ground, and extend themselves, more and more, while they followed up the Russian battalions that had been thrown forward.

The first Austrian battalions made their attack on the enemy with coolness and intrepidity, although they were entirely composed of new levies. They fell upon a French regiment which had been the first to advance on the crest of the hill, and which was nearly surrounded. The French received the Austrians with firmness, and defended themselves with valour, notwithstanding which they were forced to retreat; but, receiving a reinforcement, they quickly regained the ground which they had lost.

Two Russian regiments, belonging to the second column, the grenadiers of Fanagorisky, and the musketeers of Rhiasky, who were left in Reserve upon the height which the column had occupied during the night, were ordered, by the general-in-chief, to reinforce the brigade under General Kamensky. The troops commanded by this general fought very bravely during the whole of this unfortunate battle. They came to the support of the Austrian brigades; and this reinforcement seemed likely to re-establish the balance of power in the attack of the crest of the hill; upon which the French generals manoeuvred their troops with that ability which is the result of a military eye, and of experience, taking advantage of the inequalities of ground to cover their troops from fire, and to conceal their movements.

There was no other chance of turning the fate of the day but a general and desperate attack at the point of the bayonet. The Austrian brigades, with that under General Kamensky, charged the enemy; the Russians shouting, according to their usual custom; but the French received them with steadiness, and a well-supported fire, which made a dreadful carnage in the compact ranks of the Russians. General Miloradovich, on his side, advanced upon the right; but the Generals Berg and Repninsky being wounded, their troops had lost that confidence in themselves, without which nothing is to be done in war. The ardour of this attack soon evaporated. The superior numbers of the enemy, and his steadiness, soon changed it to a slow uncertain pace, accompanied by an ill-directed fire of musketry.

Nevertheless, the example of some of their officers had at one moment the effect of inducing the left wing again to advance with intrepidity; and, for an instant, the right wing of the French began to give way. The regiment of Salzbourg, and the battalion of Auersperg, fought with much courage.

****

> *Note by a French Officer.*—It is very true, that the Austrians fought well, as asserted by the Austrian officer; as also that the regiment of Salzbourg particularly distinguished itself, and lost a great number of men by the bayonet.

****

Kamensky's Brigade always distinguished itself. The Austrian general, Jurczeck, was severely wounded. The enemy, well aware of the importance of this post, now in turn attacked the Allies, who were without any support whatever, and absolutely abandoned by the left of the army. The fourth column now lost the heights of Pratzen, beyond the possibility of recovery, together with the greatest part of its artillery, which was entangled in the deep clay that prevails in that part of the country. The greatest possible efforts were made to repair the confusion incident to such a retreat.

Meanwhile, the enemy had advanced his artillery, and vigorously plied it in cannonading the Allies during their retreat, which put the finishing stroke to the disorder they were in. The Austrian part of this column had one general, six superior officers, nineteen subalterns, and 1,886 soldiers killed and wounded; five officers and 470 soldiers taken prisoners. This action, upon the heights of Pratzen, lasted about two hours; after which the fate of the battle was decided. The fourth column marched upon Waschan, and repaired (as pointed out in the disposition) to the position of Hodiegitz and Herspitz, where it collected its battalions.

The enemy, being once in possession of the heights, did not disturb this retreat, and remained near Pratzen, waiting, probably, the event of the 'movements on the left of the Allies. After the unfortunate attack that was made by the *Hulans*, Lieutenant-General Prince John de Liechtenstein, with his cavalry, covered the country between Blasowitz and Pratzen. The Austrian general, Caramelli, made a charge with the *Cuirassiers* of the regiment of Lorraine upon the enemy's infantry, which coming out of Girschikowitz took advantage of the vineyards between that village and Pratzen, to take the Russians in flank.

This attack, in which General Caramelli had his horse shot under him, had the effect of checking the French for a moment. The major who commanded the regiment, a Count d'Auersperg, was killed. Prince John de Liechtenstein also caused an attack to be made on the French infantry, by the regiment of Nassau, at which time the fourth column had already lost the heights of Pratzen, and was put to the route. Prince John de Liechtenstein flew to its assistance to cover the retreat with the remains of the cavalry.

This general tried to rally some Austrian battalions, which, like the Russian infantry, were retreating in disorder, and was successful in his efforts. His horse was killed under him by a grape-shot. The cavalry continued to occupy the bottom of the heights of Pratzen, between that village and Krzenowitz, till it was night.

While the action took this turn on the heights of Pratzen, and the cavalry under Prince John de Liechtenstein attempted to make head, both to the right and left, against the enemy's infantry, and a part of Prince Murat's cavalry, in order to check, or at least retard, the success of the French. The grand duke, Constantine, also found himself engaged in an obstinate contest. The village of Blasowitz, which he had caused to be occupied, as we have before seen, was attacked, and carried by the corps under Marshal Bernadotte. The grand duke wishing to check the enemy's progress, left the commanding heights on which he was posted, and advanced in line upon the enemy's columns. A sharp fire of musketry ensued.

The French sharp-shooters, who covered the columns, disputed their ground; but were at length driven in by a charge with the bayonet, which was ordered by the grand duke. A sharp cannonade, attended with much execution, then took place on this point. The grape-shot made a dreadful carnage; but, at the moment when the prince approached the enemy, (who had by this time deployed into line) the cavalry of the guards, commanded by Marshal Bessières, which had been posted in the intervals of the infantry, made a charge on the Russian line, which, being without support, was in consequence driven back, after a brave resistance.

The grand duke's regiment of horse-guards, in order to disengage the infantry, made a charge on the enemy's flank, where it checked and routed their cavalry, and afterwards attacked the French infantry, which had advanced to support the cavalry. It was on this occasion that the regiment of horse-guards captured a French eagle belonging to a battalion of the fourth regiment. The corps of guards being obliged to retire, succeeded, after considerable loss, in rallying and forming its battalions on the heights which it had originally quitted; from whence it continued its movement upon Austerlitz, marching towards Krzenowitz.

The enemy's cavalry again returned to the charge, but was checked by the horse-guards, and some squadrons of hussars belonging to the guards, who attacked the French with the greatest impetuosity at the very moment when they were about to charge the infantry during its retreat. The horse-guards valiantly attacked, and were closely engaged with the French horse grenadier guards, who, under the command of General Rapp, had arrived to reinforce the enemy's cavalry.

From that moment the Russian guards effected their retreat upon Austerlitz, without farther molestation from the French, who remained on the heights in front of Blasowitz. Prince Repnin, a colonel of the horse-guards, was wounded and made prisoner, with some officers of the same corps. The Russian guards suffered severely, but had few taken prisoners.

While these things were passing on the left, Prince Bagration, it has been already stated, had advanced in front of Posorsitz, and had tried to occupy the heights of Dwaroschna. Lieutenant-General Uwarrow, with the cavalry under his command, was upon that prince's left, near Holubitz; which village, as well as that of Krug, had been occupied in the manner before described; but Marshal Lannes arriving with his troops in column on Prince Bagration's left, and on the right of the cavalry under General Uwarrow, put a stop to the march of the right of the Allies.

In order to cover the left of the French Army, and to secure its retreat in case of disaster, Marshal Lannes had posted eighteen pieces of cannon, protected by the Twenty-Seventh regiment of Infantry, upon the commanding height, situated between Lesch and Kowalowitz, to the left of the causeway leading to Brünn: it was the same height that was to have been occupied by Prince Bagration. This general was under the necessity of reinforcing his left (on which a heavy cannonade was opened), and of sending almost the whole of his cavalry to General Uwarrow, who, in consequence, had about thirty squadrons under his orders.

The enemy succeeded, notwithstanding, in driving back General Ulanius from the villages of Krug and Holubitz, and continued to advance in column; their march being protected by a part of the cavalry under Prince Murat. This gave occasion to some fine charges on the part of both the Russian and French cavalry. General Ulanius, who commanded the cavalry with the greatest degree of intelligence and bravery, succeeded by his efforts in checking the rapid progress which the enemy would otherwise have made on the right of the Allies. Prince Bagration, after having long maintained himself at Posorsitz, retired upon the heights of Rausnitz, at the moment when the Russian guards were quitting the heights in rear of Blasowitz; and, in the evening, received orders to march to Austerlitz.

The high road to Wischau was in consequence left entirely uncovered, on which the chief part of the baggage of the army was afterwards captured by the enemy. Lieutenant-General Uwarrow, with the cavalry, protected this retreat; and Prince Bagration took post in rear of Austerlitz, at six o'clock in the evening, while the cavalry under Prince John de Liechtenstein still continued to occupy the heights in front of that place.

It now becomes necessary to revert to what was passing at Tellnitz and Sokolnitz. The first, second, and third columns, were left in the act of marching upon the points of attack fixed in the primary disposition, without thinking of the enemy's movements, and without having discrimination enough to give that direction to their columns, which the nature of the ground and the position of the enemy ought to have pointed out, at the very first glance. These three columns were composed of fifty-five battalions (without including the brigade under General Kamensky, which had not followed them), and were only opposed to the division under Legrand, not above five or six thousand strong, and to four thousand of the corps under Marshal Davoust.

★★★★★★★★★★

Note by a French officer.—General Legrand had only one of his brigades with him; the other, commanded by General Levasseur, was posted in reserve, in front of the rivulet, and of the village of Hobesnitz, from whence it marched on the flank and rear of the enemy, when he attempted to retake the heights of Pratzen; it was this unforeseen movement which greatly contributed to the defeat of that column. Levasseur's brigade fought during the remainder of the day, in conjunction with the divisions of St. Hilaire and Vandamme.

✯✯✯✯✯✯✯✯✯✯

Had the left of the Allied Army observed the enemy's movements during the battle, and reflected upon his intentions; had it taken advantage of the ground, and seized the means which it presented for again concentrating itself, in order to execute a bold manoeuvre by the height on which the chapel above Aujest is situated, and which extends quite to Pratzen. Had this been done, the battle might yet have been prolonged, and at least have given a chance that the event of this day would have been less decisive. The offensive movement on the part of the French disconcerted the attack of the Allies; and, from that moment, all concert ceased.

The second and third columns were left in Sokolnitz, through which the head of the latter had passed. It was also stated, that the two columns had become entangled during a thick fog that took place, and they were thrown into confusion, in this village, where they mutually embarrassed each other. At this time that part of the French which had been engaged in front of Tellnitz retired upon Sokolnitz; General Legrand having ordered that village to be turned by General Franceschi. When this took place, the centre of the Allies had already been penetrated; and the French were in possession of the heights of Pratzen.

The Russians who were in Sokolnitz, and those who had passed through it, when they saw themselves surrounded, immediately surrendered. Lieutenant-General Przibischewsky, who had the command of the third column, was made prisoner in the valley of Sokolnitz, together with 6,000 men, being a part of both columns, which likewise lost the whole of their artillery.

The relics of the second column retreated in disorder upon Aujest, and what continued embodied fell back upon the first column. This latter, informed, when too late, of the attack made by the French upon the centre, intended to move to its support; but took a wrong direction to be capable of making a diversion in its favour. The Austrian cavalry, which had been left beyond

Tellnitz, retired through that village, which was now evacuated, leaving some battalions of infantry, with a few cavalry on the hill fronting it, as a corps of observation, and to secure the march of M. de Buxhoevden, who was retiring upon Aujest, by the same route he had advanced.

To protect the flank of the Russian infantry, the Szeckler hussars under Prince Maurice Liechtenstein, and O'Reilly's light cavalry, with two regiments of Cossacks, under General Stutterheim, were advanced upon the plain, between the foot of the mountains and the villages of Tellnitz and Sokolnitz; General Nostitz, with the hussars of Hesse Homburg, marched with the column, the French, after their success in the centre, had already brought forward their reserve, consisting of 20 battalions, and had extended along the crest of the heights that were occupied in the morning by the Allies, from Pratzen to the chapel above Aujest, but, as yet, they were not in force, and had no cannon above that village.

****

Note by a French officer.—The first column had no longer the means of resuming the offensive. The reserve, composed of 20 battalions of grenadiers, had reached the heights in rear of the divisions St. Hilaire and Vandamme. (The emperor, with the cavalry belonging to the guards, was already descending from the chapel of St. Anthony.) The rear of the column was exposed to Marshal Davoust and General Legrand. Marshal Bernadotte, *alone*, had 18 battalions, not one half of which had burnt priming, and the remainder had been but little engaged.

The French would have gained the victory with 25,000 men less than they had, which is a subject of reflection for military men, and sufficiently shews the influence which the being well commanded has over the operations, of war.

****

If the first column of the Allies, reinforced by some battalions from the second, and at that time consisting of above 30 battalions, had moved in full force upon these heights, and had attacked them; if, instead of passing through a defile, (the height above which was occupied by the enemy,) it had made a charge on the flank of the French, it is possible that a diversion might have been effected in favour of the centre; and a defeat in Aujest (which was to be anticipated) would at least have been avoided. In marching upon the height above Aujest, the left of the Allies might, at least, give a chance in favour of the battle; while the left, being no longer liable to be put in confusion, would not have lost so many men. Even supposing it not to have succeeded in maintaining the height, still it had always a retreat open upon Scharoditz.

As soon as the column arrived in Aujest, the French rushed like a torrent down upon the village, in which a sharp fire of musketry at first took place, but which was of short duration, before they gained possession of the village. It was the division of Vandamme, which had formed the extreme right, on the heights of Pratzen, and which, in proportion as the French crowned that height, had gradually moved upon the chapel, above Aujest. The general of infantry, Buxhoevden, with a few battalions, succeeded in passing through the village, and rejoined the army near Austerlitz; some confusion took place, and 4,000 men were taken prisoners in or about Aujest: they also lost their artillery.

Many of the fugitives betook themselves to the lake, which was frozen over, but not sufficiently so to prevent many from perishing in it. The enemy, who in the meantime had received his artillery, vigorously plied the fugitives with it, who afterwards passed through Satschan, and in the evening succeeded in regaining the rear-guard of the army, on the heights of Neuhof. After the French had occupied Aujest, the centre and rear of the first column, which was so very strong, fell back under the orders of Lieut.-General Dochtorow, upon the plain between Tellnitz and the lake. This infantry was collected, but not in good order.

Lieut.-General Dochtorow succeeded for a moment in re-establishing order, after which he considered only how to effect his retreat. This was very difficult in the execution, and could only be effected across a very narrow dike between the lakes, on which it was not possible to march more than two men in front. There was also reason to apprehend that the French passing by Aujest and Satschan, round the lake, would thus cut off the dike, the only retreat now left to the Russians, which would have made it impossible to save this last wreck of the left wing of the Allied Army. Lieut.-General Kienmayer, with the hussars of Hesse Hombourg, was sent over in advance, for the purpose of securing this retreat, and posted himself upon the heights between Satschan and Ottnitz, in order to observe this point.

Meanwhile, the Austrian cavalry continued to support General Dochtorow, and for that purpose advanced into the plain, between Aujest and Sokolnitz. The generals who commanded O'Reilly's light cavalry and the Szeckler hussars, advanced to the attack of two French regiments of dragoons, who approached from Sokolnitz, but seeing that the Russian infantry was supported, the latter marched by their left, upon the height near Aujest, and posted themselves at the head of the division of Vandamme.

The conclusion of this battle was very remarkable, since the French troops of the right wing were turning their backs upon Austerlitz to attack the remains of the left of the Allies; to do which, the French were now quitting the same heights, whence the Allies had marched in the morning, to attack them. When the first column had advanced, the lake was the point of appuy to the right of the French; at *this* moment it was the appuy to their *left*, while the Russians had their right upon it.

It was now about two o'clock in the afternoon; the action was decided and finished along the rest of the line, when the division of Vandamme advanced to complete it. In rear of Tellnitz, between that village and Menitz, was a hill of considerable elevation, the right of which was on the lake. To this hill the Russian infantry retired, still under the protection of the Austrian cavalry, which was every instant mowed down by discharges of grape-shot.

The village of Tellnitz, which has already been described as surrounded by ditches, presented the means of defence, which were taken advantage of; and to give time to the rest of the column to file off, a regiment of Russian infantry, under Major

General Lewis, was posted behind these ditches, where it was attacked, but defended itself with resolution.

From that time, General Dochtorow continued his retreat. The cavalry occupied the hill that has been mentioned, in order to save a great part of this column, which was again in the greatest possible confusion. The French got possession of Tellnitz (in which a great many Russian stragglers were taken prisoners), and bringing the light artillery of the guards down to the edge of the lake, for the purpose of driving the Austrian cavalry from their post on the hill, they opened a fire on the flank of O'Reilly's light cavalry, and destroyed a great part of it. Yet nothing could prevent this brave regiment from continuing to cover the retreat of the Russians with the greatest intrepidity.

Colonel Degenfeldt posted his light artillery, which commanded that of the French, with so much judgment as to damp the ardour of their fire. The Colonel of the Szeckler hussars was desperately wounded in the head with a grape-shot.

The Russian infantry, fatigued and exhausted, retired very slowly, and the cavalry had a long time to support their post; at length, however, this famous dike, the only remaining retreat to the wreck of the first column of the Allies, and which had justly been the subject of so much uneasiness, was happily passed; still, however, the French (who occupied the hill, before in possession of the cavalry, as soon as they quitted it) continued to fire on them, with their artillery, till they were completely out of reach.

Having passed the dike, the two Austrian generals, who protected General Dochtorow's retreat, halted on the heights in front of Neuhoff, and tried to restore order in the Russian Battalions, which yet formed a corps of at least 8,000 men.

It was then about four o'clock, and already began to grow dark. The retreat was then continued by Boschowitz; the troops marched the whole night, under a heavy fall of rain, which completed the destruction of the roads; the remaining artillery sunk in the sloughs, and were abandoned. The Austrian cavalry formed the rear guard, without being pursued by the French, who halted on the dike. The regiment of O'Reilly brought off its artillery.

The French Army took up the position occupied by the' Allied Army the preceding night; the latter, after the greatest exertion on the part of the two emperors to remedy the general confusion on the field of battle, retired in the evening completely behind Austerlitz, into the position of Hodiegitz. But the very considerable loss it had sustained in killed and wounded, and the number of those who were prisoners, or missing; more especially of the first, second, third, and fourth columns, made this army, on its arrival in rear of Austerlitz, in a very feeble state; at least, as far as regards its disposable force.

The Austrian cavalry, commanded by General Prince Hohenlohe, (who was sent to replace Prince John de Liechtenstein that same night, on the latter being charged with a mission to the Emperor Napoleon:) this cavalry, alone, had some detachments in front of Austerlitz, and formed the rear guard of the army. Thus, closed this ever-memorable day.

Should any errors of detail have crept into the foregoing narrative, those military men who have been engaged in actual service will know how to make allowances for them; they will know, from experience, how difficult it is to procure exact information, as to the minute particulars of a great battle. Two persons rarely see the same object in a similar point of view. But, as to the general arrangement, the plans, and the principal movements, their execution, and their result, my pen has been strictly guided by the love of truth, an accurate knowledge of what was done, and the utmost impartiality.

It will not have escaped the observation of the experienced soldier, that it is principally to the following causes that the loss of this battle is to be attributed. To the want of correctness in the information possessed by the Allies, as to the enemy's army; to the bad plan of attack, supposing the enemy to have been entrenched in a position which he did not occupy; to the movements executed the day before the attack, and in sight of the enemy, in order to gain the right flank of the French; to the great interval between the columns when they quitted the heights of Pratzen; and to their want of communication with each other. To these causes may be attributed the first misfortunes of the Austro-Russian Army.

But, in spite of these capital errors, it would still have been possible to restore the fortune of the day, in favour of the Allies, if the second and third columns had thought less of the primary disposition, and attended more to the enemy, who, by the boldness of his manoeuvre, completely overthrew the basis on which the plan of attack was founded; or, if the first column (which possessed the means of doing so), instead of retiring by Aujest, as before mentioned, had marched to the assistance of the two former, and, together with them (or at least with what remained of them) had moved upon the heights, of which the French had as yet but a precarious possession, so long as the left of the Allies was unbroken, and their extreme right, which made only feeble demonstrations, continued at Posorsitz.

No computation has been made in this work, as to the loss of the two armies, at the battle of Austerlitz. It is impossible for anyone, though actually bearing a part in the action, to calculate with any degree of accuracy the number of killed and wounded on each side.

The carnage made on the 2nd December was very great. The few Austrian troops there yet remained were not collected on one point; but, as we have seen, conducted themselves everywhere with constancy and animation. The sixth battalions of the regiments of Wurtemberg and Reuss-Graitz were the only corps that were in confusion at the time when the fourth column was defeated. The Russians, at the commencement, fought with intrepidity, and the guards and *Hulans* distinguished themselves for their courage.

The French infantry manoeuvred with coolness and precision, fought with courage, and executed its bold movements with admirable concert. After having made some efforts, without effect, the Russian Battalions began to waver; confusion and, finally, complete defeat were the consequences of the imprudent conduct of the second and third columns.

The fourth column of the Allies abandoned a *part* of its artillery. The first, second, and third columns, lost the *whole* of theirs, with the exception of General Kienmayer's corps, which saved its cannon. The guns were entangled in the sloughs, as before mentioned, and the Russian horses, which are more calculated for speed than for draft, could not drag them out of the deep clay, into which they had sunk. The number of the Russian prisoners may be computed at 15,000 men; while their killed and wounded must have been very considerable; in addition to which, as always happens on such occasions, they had a great number of soldiers missing.

The loss of the French Army must also, necessarily, have been very considerable. The fire, at the commencement of the action, was too warmly kept up, not to have done great execution; still, however, the French force was by no means diminished in the same proportion as that of the Allies. The generals who were killed, wounded, and taken prisoners are already well known.

The 3rd and 4th of December

The Austro-Russian Army had experienced so many difficulties in regard to its subsistence, on the line of operations it had followed previous to these offensive movements, that it was abandoned, during the retreat, in order to direct its march upon Hungary. The Allies quitted the position of Hodiegitz at 12 o'clock at night, and marched upon Czeitsch, where they arrived on the morning of the third of December. The column under General Dochtorow arrived at Niskowitz, on the road to Hungary, where it found General Kienmayer then forming the rear-guard of the Allies.

★★★★★★★★★★

Note by a French officer.—It is too ridiculous to suppose that the Russian Army, without artillery, without baggage, and without provisions, would have preferred a retreat by its flank (which exposed it to the danger of being surrounded by the French Army) to that upon Olmutz: but, in the course of this day, it lost its line of operation, which was the high road to Olmutz, and nothing remained for it but to move upon Goeding; and it did not gain much by that; for, had it not been for the too great clemency of the emperor, and the armistice, which was concluded, the remains of the Russian Army would have been entirely destroyed; as may be perceived from what the Austrian officer lets fall a little farther on.—The loss of a battle is no proof of want of talent in a general: but the loss of his artillery and baggage, of his line of operations, and his retreat, are positive evidence that he is ignorant of the art of war.
An army, so commanded, never could make head against a French Army in so great and difficult a warfare. The emperor

took advantage of the faults committed by the enemy, who would have committed yet greater errors had the emperor retired behind Brünn: the latter would have been in greater force; and had already planned new combinations, in the course of which, the general who possessed most experience, and the greatest genius for the art of war, must naturally have taken his adversary at a disadvantage.

****

This Russian column continued its march, for the purpose of rejoining the army at Czeitsch; but lost a considerable number of men during the night, who had straggled and lost themselves in the woods and villages. The Austrian cavalry, which had protected the retreat of these wrecks of the left wing of the combined army, and which was a part of the corps under M. de Kienmayer, halted at Niskowitz. Lieut.-General Prince Bagration was a league in rear of this Austrian corps, occupying the heights of Urschutz. Between Niskowitz and Urschutz is a large wood, under cover of which, the French had it in their power to surround and cut off the corps under M. de Kienmayer, which was thus too much pushed forward.

He therefore remained in this position no longer than was necessary to give time to the stragglers of the army, and to some baggage to fall back upon Urschutz, and to obtain some knowledge of the enemy's movements. As soon as the French, who had entered Austerlitz in the morning, began to advance, General Kienmayer fell back upon General Bagration, and in front of Saruschitz formed the support of that prince's corps. A detachment of O'Reilly's light cavalry, and some Cossacks, were sent to Stanitz, to watch that road. The corps under M. de Merveldt had received orders to retire from Lunenbourg, in the direction of Goeding, to observe the country on the left, and principally the two roads of Auspitz and Nicolsbourg.

On the third of December, the French Army advanced in the following manner:

The cavalry, under Prince Murat, which had pushed forward detachments upon Rausnitz and Wischau (on the evening of the same day on which the battle was fought) pursued that route, and made immense booty: it advanced beyond Prosnitz, and then sent out strong detachments upon Kremsir.

Marshal Lannes at first took the same road, and then moved by his right, to gain the right of the Allies by Butschowitz and Stanitz. Marshals Soult and Bernadotte, the imperial guards, and the grenadiers of the reserve, were posted on the route towards Hungary, as soon as the Emperor Napoleon had received information of the direction taken by the Allied Army; they advanced, however, but slowly; probably with a view to give time to the extreme right of their army to gain ground on the left of the Allies.

Marshal Davoust marched upon the left flank of the Austro-Russian Army, by the route of Nicolsbourg, (in which was the division of Gudin,) and by that of Auspitz, in which was the remainder of that corps; these two roads unite within half a league of Goeding.

Prince Bagration had placed some outposts in the wood of Urschutz. The French, about two o'clock in the afternoon, began to reconnoitre it, obtained possession of the wood, and established themselves on the skirts of it. A trifling affair ensued, which lasted about two hours, and which terminated by General Bagration maintaining his post, which, however, he evacuated that evening, retiring towards Czeitsch; General Kienmayer posted himself in his front, upon the heights of Nasedlowitz, pushing forward his outposts in the direction of Urschutz.

The 4th of December the Allied Army crossed the River March, and arrived at Hollitsch, much diminished in numbers, and with very few effectives, compared with the army to which it was opposed. The Emperor Alexander took up his quarters in the castle of Hollitsch, while the Emperor of Germany remained at Czeitsch, to be ready for the interview which was about to take place with the Emperor Napoleon.

An armistice had been agreed on, to take place at daybreak on the 4th December. Prince John de Liechtenstein had returned from the headquarters of the French the evening before with this intelligence. But their advanced guard, probably from not having received timely orders on this subject, advanced to attack the fore-posts of M. de Kienmayer's corps, which remained upon the heights of Nasedlowitz. Prince Bagration then retired quite behind Czeitsch. However, this misunderstanding, and the firing consequent upon it, were soon put a stop to. A suspension of arms took place, and the space of about a league and a half was left between the outposts of the two armies. That of the French had advanced, and taken up its position in several lines, between Damborschutz, and Saruschutz, in front of Urschutz.

It was then that the famous interview, which gave peace to the two empires, took place between the Emperor Francis II. and Napoleon; it passed at a little distance from the village of Nasedlowitz, near a mill, by the side of the high-road, and in the open air. The conversation of these two sovereigns lasted some time, when the Emperor of Germany returned to Czeitsch, which he reached in the evening, and immediately set about informing his ally of the result of the interview—For this purpose, an Austrian general was to be sent immediately to Hollitsch; and General Savary, *aide-de-camp* to the Emperor Napoleon, was named by his sovereign, in the first instance to attend the Emperor Francis II. and afterwards to accompany the general that should be sent to Hollitsch.

In case His Majesty, the Emperor of all the Russias, should consent to the conditions of the armistice, General Savary was empowered to countermand the march of Marshal Davoust's corps, and was afterwards to accompany the Austrian general, to acquaint the corps of M. de Merveldt with the suspension of arms. General Stutterheim, who was with the rear-guard of the corps, near which the interview took place, was charged by his sovereign with this commission.

It was twelve o'clock at night before these two generals reached Hollitsch, where they had the happiness of obtaining immediate access to the presence of the Emperor Alexander, who received them with kindness, and threw no obstacle in the way of the armistice.

Upon this they again departed immediately to find out the

corps under M. de Merveldt, and to countermand that under Marshal Davoust: the former they fell in with at two o'clock in the morning, retiring upon Goeding. M. de Merveldt, we have already seen, was charged with the protection of the left flank of the Russian Army; but the whole force under his orders did not exceed 4,000 infantry and 500 cavalry, which made it impossible for him to impede the march of the right of the French Army.

The two generals succeeded in falling in with Marshal Davoust at Josephsdorf, at about four o'clock in the morning. General Gudin's advanced guard was at Neudorf. According to the agreement between the Emperor Francis II. and Napoleon, all the troops remained in the exact situation in which they were found upon the cessation of hostilities being made known to them.

The following day Prince John de Liechtensten returned to Austerlitz (which was the headquarter of the Emperor Napoleon) for the purpose of negotiating the boundary to be observed by the respective armies during the continuation of the armistice which preceded the peace concluded between Austria and France.

On the 4th December, the very day on which the armistice took place, the Archduke Ferdinand, who could not be made acquainted with it, and who had received orders to advance and observe the Bavarians that remained at Iglau, after the departure of Marshal Bernadotte: on this day, that prince attacked General Wrede (to keep him in check) with some troops, the remnant of his corps; with which he succeeded in driving him from Iglau.

The Archduke Charles, obliged to retreat in consequence of the unheard-of catastrophe that happened to the German Army, arrived in Hungary, with his army quite entire, after having at Caldiero incapacitated the French Army of Italy from doing him any mischief.

It appears, then, that wherever their generals allowed the Austrian troops to fight, they fought well; and it would be a very rash, and a very false opinion, to impute the misfortunes of the war of 1805 to them. In that, as well as in all former instances, the Austrian Army distinguished itself by its courage, its devotion to the cause, its constancy in supporting unheard of privations, and by its implicit obedience. It was at Ulm that these brave troops, victims to the conduct of M. Mack, were subjected to that heart-breaking fate which was the destruction of the German Army. But, at Ulm, many regiments that had not fired a single shot were obliged to surrender, in consequence of the operations pursued, and in pursuance of orders given by that M. Mack, who talked of *burying himself in the ruins of Ulm; who always talked of death, yet feared to die.*

Ulm and Austerlitz

Montgomery B. Gibbs

Napoleon had now reached such a point of power that the Bourbons resigned all hopes of restoration through his agency, and as the next best means of obtaining control of the throne of France assassination was decided upon.

The First Consul had scarcely been in Paris a month, after the engagement at Marengo when Ceracchi, a sculptor of some fame, attempted Bonaparte's life as he was entering the theatre. But for his betrayal by a co-conspirator the plot would have succeeded. This attempt by means of the dagger was followed by the explosion of an infernal machine, which consisted of a barrel of gunpowder surrounded by an immense quantity of grape shot. On the night of October 10th the machine was placed at Nacaise, a narrow street through which Napoleon was to pass on his way to the opera house.

Some years later, in telling of the narrow escape he had on that night, he said:

> I had been hard at work all day, and was so overpowered by sleep after dinner that Josephine, who was quite anxious to go to the opera that night, found it quite difficult to arouse me and persuade me to go. I fell asleep again after we had entered the carriage, and I was dreaming of the danger I had undergone some years before in crossing the Tagliamento at midnight by the light of torches, during a flood, when I was waked by the explosion of the infernal machine. 'We are blown up,' I said to Bessières and Lannes, who were in the carriage, and then quickly commanded

the coachman to drive on.

The coachman, who was intoxicated, heard the order, and having mistaken the explosion for a salute, lashed his horses furiously until the theatre was reached. The machine had been fired by a slow match, and the explosion took place just twenty seconds too soon. Summary justice was executed upon the perpetrators of this infamous deed, and sometime later the Duke d'Enghien atoned for the part, whatever it might have been, that the Bourbons had taken in these murderous schemes.

Austria delayed for several months final negotiations of the treaty agreed upon after the engagement at Marengo, evidently reassured by the attempts made on the First Consul's life. Preliminaries of peace had been signed at Paris, between the Austrian general, Saint Julian, and the French government. Duroc was dispatched to the Emperor of Austria, to obtain his ratification of the articles; but having reached the headquarters of the Army of the Rhine, he was refused a pass to proceed on his journey.

Napoleon immediately ordered Moreau to recommence hostilities, unless the emperor delivered up the fortresses of Ulm, Ingolstadt and Phillipsburg as pledges of his sincerity. Austria, accordingly, purchased a further protraction of the armistice at this heavy price; at the same time offering to treat for peace on new grounds. News of the occupation of the three fortresses by the French troops, was announced in Paris on the 23rd of September 1800, where the fresh hopes of peace caused universal satisfaction.

These hopes, however, proved delusive. Austria delayed and equivocated, until it became evident the emperor would make no peace separate from England, and that the latter power was prepared to support her ally.

Napoleon, perceiving that he was being trifled with, now gave orders (in November, 1800) to all his generals to put their divisions in march all along the frontiers of the French dominions. The shock was instantaneous, from the Rhine to the Mincio. Brune overwhelmed the Austrians on the Mincio; Macdonald held the Tyrol, and Moreau achieved the glorious victory of Hohenlinden after a desperate and most sanguinary battle.

This latter contest decided the fate of the campaign. Thus, with three victorious armies, either of which could have marched triumphantly into Vienna, Napoleon hesitated long enough before taking that final step, to allow Austria to sign an honest and definite peace.

The treaty of Luneville was at last signed in good faith on February 9th, 1801. By the peace of Luneville, Napoleon for the second time effected the pacification of the Continent. Of all the powerful coalition which threatened France in 1800, England alone continued hostile in 1801 if we except Turkey, with which no arrangement could be made until the affairs of Egypt were settled.

On the 8th of March, 1801, a British Army of 17,000 men landed in Egypt under the command of Sir Ralph Abercromby. The French were very ill-prepared for an attack. The English Army overcame the resistance of the forces which opposed their landing through the heavy surf formed on the beach, and advanced upon their enemy. No general action occurred until the 21st when the English obtained a decisive victory and drove Menou—who had succeeded to the command of the troops in Egypt at the death of Kléber—with great loss within the walls of Alexandria.

Here he was blockaded and General Belliard, cut off from all communication with him, capitulated after which Menou submitted. Each capitulated, on condition of being taken back to France with all his troops and their arms and baggage. Thus ended the conquest of Egypt by Napoleon. The French admiral, Gantheaume, had long been making fruitless efforts to land reinforcements in Egypt, but had been unable to elude the British ships. He was now ordered to return to Toulon, where preparations were made to receive the French troops.

After the news of the reverses of the French Army in Egypt, and the great sea victory of Copenhagen by Nelson, Napoleon was determined to bring England to negotiations of peace and a recognition of the French Republic, and with this in view he gathered an army of 100,000 men on the coasts of France, with a flotilla sufficiently large to effect a landing in England, whenever circumstances seemed to favour such a movement.

At this very moment it was, that Fulton, the inventor of steamboats, communicated his discovery to the First Consul. Napoleon thus had the first chance placed in his hands of possessing exclusively for a time, the greatest and most diversified means of physical power ever known in the world. Scarcely deigning to bestow a thought upon the subject the First Consul treated the inventor as a "visionary."

Whether or not Napoleon ever intended to invade Great Britain, he succeeded at all events in convincing the world for a time that such was his design, and when the peace of Amiens was signed on March 25th, 1802, Paris and London rejoiced, as did all civilized nations. The peace of Amiens left the military resources of France unemployed on the hands of Bonaparte. This induced him to think of profiting by the European calm, and effect the conquest of St. Domingo. He gave the command of the expedition to his brother-in-law, Leclerc; but it was unsuccessful.

The inauguration of Christian worship once more in France in 1802 gave Napoleon an opportunity to show that he had the interest of the people at heart. France was an *infidel* nation, and it was the fashion to believe there was no God. The signing of the Concordat by Pope Pius VII. gave to France what she had long needed—a form of religious worship. It required no little strength of purpose to take this step. Napoleon said:

> Religion is a principle which cannot be eradicated from the heart of man. Last Sunday I was walking here alone, and the church bells of the village of Ruel rang at sunset. I was strongly moved, so vividly did the memory of early days come back with that sound. If it be thus with me, what must it be with others? In re-establishing the Church, I consult the wishes of the great majority of my people.

A grand religious ceremony took place at Notre Dame Cathedral to celebrate the proclamation of the Concordat, at which the First Consul presided with great pomp, attended by all the ministers and general officers then in Paris. Another measure, adopted at this period, was the decree permitting the return of the emigrants, provided they appeared and took the oath to the government within a certain period. It is estimated that a hundred thousand exiles returned to their country in consequence of this decree.

It was about this period, too, that the First Consul turned his attention to the system of a national education, He also commenced the herculean task of preparing a code of law for the French nation with the result that the "Code Napoleon" is known to every civilized nation of the earth. Public improvements, formerly projected, were now carried out, and sciences and the arts progressed as never before.

The order of the Legion of Honour owes its inception to Napoleon Bonaparte, and it was he who placed it on such a footing in France that it has since thrived there as has no similar institution on the Continent. When established by him, after months of careful consideration, he believed it necessary to France. To his Counsellors of State, he said:

> They talk about ribbons and crosses being the playthings of monarchs, and say that the old Romans had no system of honorary rewards. The Romans had patricians, knights, citizens and slaves—for each class different dresses and different manners—mural crowns, civic crowns, orations, triumphs and titles. When the noble band of patricians lost its influence, Rome fell to pieces—the people were a vile rabble. It was then that you saw the fury of Marius, the proscriptions of Scylla, and afterward of the emperors. In that manner Brutus is talked of as the enemy of tyrants; he was an aristocrat, who stabbed Caesar because Caesar wished to lower the authority of the senate. You call these ribbons and crosses child's rattles—be it so: It is with such rattles that men are led. I would not say that to the multitude, but in a council of wise men and statesmen one may speak the truth . . . Observe how the people bow before the decorations of foreigners.
>
> Voltaire calls the common soldiers 'Alexanders at five *sous* a day.' He was right. It is just so. Do you imagine you

can make men fight by reasoning? Never! You must bribe them with glory, with distinctions and rewards. In fine, it is agreed that we have need of some kind of institutions. If this Legion of Honour is not approved, let some other be suggested. I do not pretend that it alone will save the State, but it will do its part.

The Legion of Honour was instituted on the 15th of May 1802. When Napoleon had seen the fruits of it, he said:

This order was the reward of everyone who was an honour to his country, stood at the head of his profession, and contributed to the national prosperity and glory. Some were dissatisfied, because the decoration was conferred alike on officers and soldiers; others, because it was given for civil and military merits indiscriminately; but if this order ever cease to be the recompense of the brave private, or be confined to military men alone, it will cease to be what I made it—the Legion of Honour.

The First Consul was, in right of his office, captain general of the legion and president of the council of administration. The nomination of all the members was for life. The grand officers were endowed with a yearly pension of upwards of $1,000. Pensions, decreasing in amount, were also affixed to the subordinate degrees of rank in the order. All the members were required to swear, upon their honour, to defend the government of France, and maintain the inviolability of Her Empire, to combat, by every lawful means against the re-establishment of feudal institutions, and to concur in maintaining the principle of liberty and equality.

On the day the order was instituted, Napoleon, by act of the Senate was appointed Consul for life. The First Consul accepted the offered prolongation from the Senate, on the condition that the opinion of the people should be consulted on the subject. The question put to them, as framed by Cambacérés and Le Brun, was: "Napoleon Bonaparte—Shall he be Consul for life?" Registers were opened in all municipalities; and the answer of the people qualified to vote was decisive. Upwards of three million five hundred thousand voted for the proposal; 8,300 against it. In the month of August Napoleon was formally declared Consul for life and a decree of the Senate immediately consolidated his power, by permitting him to appoint his successor.

This personal elevation had its ample share in contributing to the number of Napoleon's enemies. In fact, it appears in some measure astonishing how any individual could persuade a whole nation, day after day, to yield him up such a portion of its rights and privileges. However, among many instances that might be adduced of his powers of persuasion, one which occurred about this period is not the least remarkable. In the beginning of the summer of 1802 some officers of rank, enthusiastic republicans, took umbrage at Napoleon's conduct, and determined to go and remonstrate with him upon the points that had given them offense, and speak their minds freely. On the evening of the same day, one of the party gave the following account of the interview:

> I do not know whence it arises, but there is a charm about that man, indescribable and irresistible. I am no admirer of his; I dislike the power to which he has risen; yet I cannot help confessing that there is something in him which seems to speak him born to command. We went into his apartment, determined to declare our minds; to expostulate with him warmly; and not to depart till our subject of complaint should be removed. But in his manner of receiving us there was a certain tact which disarmed us in a moment; nor could we utter one word of what we had intended to say.
>
> He talked to us for a length of time, with an eloquence peculiarly his own, explaining with the utmost clearness and precision, the necessity of steadily pursuing the line of conduct he had adopted, and, without contradicting us in direct terms, controverted our opinions so ably, that we had not a word to offer in reply, we therefore retired, having done nothing but listen to, instead of expostulating with him, fully convinced, at least for the moment, that he was right, and that we were altogether in the wrong!

Towards the close of the year 1802 it became evident that the peace of Amiens was based on a hollow foundation, and was destined at no distant period to be overthrown. At an interview held with Lord Whitworth, an ambassador from England, Napoleon said:

> No consideration on earth shall make me consent to your retention of Malta; I would as soon agree to put you in possession of the Faubourg St, Antoine. Every wind that blows from England brings nothing but hatred and hostility towards me. An invasion is the only means of offense that I can take against her, and I am determined to put myself at the head of the expedition. There are a hundred chances to one against my success; but I am not the less determined to attempt the descent, if war must be the consequence of the present discussion.

He now quickly brought matters to a crisis. He attacked the ambassador in vigorous language at a diplomatic meeting at the Tuileries which ended in an abrupt termination of the conference by Napoleon leaving the room.

The armistice lasted until March 18th, 1803, when England again declared war upon France. All commerce of the French nation was ordered seized, wherever found, and two hundred vessels, containing at least $15,000,000 worth of property fell into the hands of England. Napoleon retaliated by arresting upwards of ten thousand Englishmen then in France. The tocsin of war was sounded in every part of Europe, and 160,000 French soldiers were marshalled on the coasts of France, again threatening an invasion of England.

France at this time was totally unprepared for war; a proof sufficient to show that the First Consul had not desired the termination of peace. The army was completely on a peace establishment; great numbers of the troops were disbanded and the parks of artillery were broken up. New plans for re-casting the artillery had been proposed, and they had already begun to break up the cannon to throw them into the furnaces. The navy was in a still less serviceable condition. In an address to the Senate Napoleon said:

> The negotiations are ended and we are attacked; let us at least fight to maintain the faith of treaties and the honour of the French name.

The nation responded with enthusiasm to the call; sums of money were voted by the large towns for building ships and the army was rapidly recruited.

The first hostile movement of Napoleon was upon the continental domains of George III. General Mortier invaded the Electorate of Hanover with 15,000 men and the Hanoverian Army laid down its arms. The second movement of the First Consul was the occupation of Naples. No resistance was attempted. These measures, besides enabling Napoleon to maintain his army by levies on the foreign states he occupied, also crippled the commerce of England by shutting up all communication with many of the best markets on the Continent. The First Consul now visited the principal towns, accompanied by Josephine, where he made observations and gave orders respecting the fortifications. These measures were all preparatory on the part of Napoleon to his determined plan to attempt the invasion of England. Funds were secured in part by the sale of Louisiana to the United States.

Assassination was now again resorted to that Napoleon might be overthrown; but every attempt, as heretofore, proved futile. Conspiracy after conspiracy was detected—all traced to Napoleon's political enemies. The First Consul resolved on retaliation and ordered the arrest of the Duke d'Enghien at his castle in the Duchy of Baden.

Three days afterwards the duke was conveyed to Paris, and after a few hours' imprisonment, was taken to the old State Prison of France, where he was tried by court martial, and in a most summary and hasty manner pronounced guilty of having fought against the Republic and condemned to death. He was led down a winding stairway by torchlight, and shot in a ditch in the castle at six o'clock in the morning. All Europe shuddered at the deed, but it produced exactly the result Napoleon intended by it; he was safe from attempts on his life forever afterwards.

Napoleon Crossing the Alps

Before the discovery of this plot the French Senate had sent an address to Napoleon congratulating him on his escape from a former conspiracy in which one hundred persons had schemed to take his life. In answer he said:

> I have long since renounced the hope of enjoying the pleasures of a private life; all my days are employed in fulfilling the duties which my fate and the will of the French people have imposed upon me. Heaven will watch over France, and defeat the plots of the wicked. The citizens may be without alarm; my life will last as long as it will be useful to the nation; but I wish the French people to understand that existence, without their confidence and affection, would be to me without consolation, and would for them have no object.

The title of First Consul, by which Napoleon had been distinguished for more than four years, was exchanged on the 18th of May 1804 for that of Emperor by the advice of the Senate, where it was first publicly broached, and by the universal assent of the French nation. Upwards of 3,500,000 voted for the measure and about 2,000 against it. The debates in the Senate were somewhat protracted and so great was the impatience of the military that the garrison of Paris had resolved to proclaim their chief as Emperor, at the first review; and Murat, governor of the city, was obliged to assemble the officers at his house, and bind them by a promise to restrain the troops.

The spirit of the army at Boulogne was soon manifested, by their voting the erection of a colossal statue of Napoleon, in bronze, to be placed in the midst of the camp. Every soldier subscribed a portion of his pay for the purpose; but there was a want of bronze. Soult, who presided over the completion of the undertaking, went, at the head of a deputation to Napoleon, and said:"Sire, lend me the bronze, and I will repay it in enemy's cannon at the first battle," and he kept his word.

On the 27th of May Napoleon received the oath of the Senate, the constituted bodies, the learned corporations and the troops of the garrison of Paris. Louis XVIII. immediately ad-

French troops crossing the St. Bernard

dressed a protest to all the sovereigns of Europe against the usurpation of Napoleon. Fouche, who was the first who heard of this document, immediately communicated the intelligence to the emperor, with a view to prepare the necessary orders to watch over those who might attempt its circulation; but great was his surprise, on receiving directions to have the whole inserted in *The Moniteur* the following morning, where it actually appeared. This was all the notice taken of the matter by Napoleon.

On December 1st of the same year, the lists of votes in favour of the establishment of the hereditary succession of the Empire in his family were publicly presented by the Senate to Napoleon, and on the following day, in the midst of one of the most imposing and brilliant scenes ever enacted in France, Napoleon and Josephine were crowned Emperor and Empress of France by Pius VII., the Pontiff of Rome, in the Cathedral of Notre Dame.

The emperor took his coronation oath as usual on such occasions, with his hand upon the Scripture, and in the form repeated to him by the Pope; but in the act of coronation itself there was a marked deviation from the universal custom. The crown having been blessed by the Pope, Napoleon took it from the altar with his own hands and placed it on his brow. He then put the diadem on the head of Josephine. The heralds proclaimed that "the thrice glorious and thrice august Napoleon, Emperor of the French, was crowned and installed;" and so ended the pageant. Sir Walter Scott say:

> Those who remember having beheld it, must now doubt whether they were waking, or whether fancy had formed a vision so dazzling in its appearance, so extraordinary in its origin and progress, and so ephemeral in its endurance."

The senators of the Italian Republic soon afterwards requested that Napoleon be crowned as their king, and on the following May 1805, in the ancient cathedral of Milan, he assumed the Iron Crown of the Lombard kings, saying as he did so, "God has given it to me; let him beware who would touch it!"

The new order of knighthood, that of the Iron Crown, with

these words for its motto, arose out of this ceremony.

On the 8th of May, while on the road to Milan, Napoleon expressed a wish to visit the battlefield of Marengo, on which he had reconquered Italy five years before. All the French troops in that part of Italy were therefore mustered there, to the number of 30,000. Covered with the hat and uniform which he wore on the day of that memorable conflict—the emperor passed the army in review on horseback, and distributed crosses of the Legion of Honour, with the same ceremonies which had been observed on the Champ de Mars and the same return of enthusiastic devotion on the parts of the troops. Bourrienne says:

> It was remarked, that the worms, who spare neither the costumes of living kings, nor the bodies of deceased heroes, had been busy with the trophies of Marengo, which, nevertheless, Bonaparte wore at the review.

Napoleon did not continue his journey until after he had laid the first stone of the monument consecrated to those who had been slain on the battlefield, and on the same day he made his entry into Milan. Meanwhile the activity in France continued unabated, and scarcely a day passed without some trifling engagement, brought on by the rigorous pursuit of the squadrons of the French fleet, as they advanced to Boulogne.

Scarcely had the emperor entered Paris after his return from the coronation in Italy, before he learned that a new coalition had been formed against him, and that England, Russia, Austria and Sweden, with half a million men, were preparing once more for war. The objects proposed were, briefly, the independence of Holland and Switzerland; the evacuation of Hanover, and the north of Germany by the French troops; the restoration of Piedmont to the King of Sardinia; and the complete evacuation of Italy by France. Great Britain, besides affording the assistance of her forces by sea and land, was to pay large subsidies for supporting the armies of the coalition. Napoleon had, in a great degree, penetrated the schemes of the allied powers, but was not prepared for the sudden assumption of arms by Austria without any declaration of war; a measure which Austria justified by re-

Inspecting the troops at Boulogne, 15th August, 1804

ferring to the increasing encroachments of France in Italy.

As the emperor desired leisure to prosecute and perfect the great public works, he had begun, or projected, he most earnestly wished for peace, and he again addressed a letter to the King of England, and which was treated with contempt. An envoy was sent to Frankfort-on-the Main to ascertain definitely whether Austria really intended to trample another treaty in the dirt, and so soon after the fatal day at Marengo. The messenger soon returned with the best maps of the German Empire, and opening them on the council table of the Tuileries, said:

> The Austrian general is advancing on Munich: the Russian Army is in motion, and Prussia will join them.

The Emperor of Russia had pushed on to Berlin to win over the Prussian monarch to the great Bourbon coalition, and to make the compact more impressive, he asked his royal brother to visit with him the tomb of Frederick the Great. They descended by torchlight to the vault, and there, over the honoured dust of Frederick, Francis, his heir, took a solemn oath, as he pointed to the sword of his ancestor as it lay on the coffin, to join the European coalition. Some weeks afterwards Napoleon visited the tomb as a conqueror, and said to his attendant, as he seized the precious relics:

> These orders and sword shall witness no other such scene of perjury over the ashes of Frederick!

The young Emperor of France now gathered his eagles to lead them toward the Danube. To the French Senate, whom Napoleon informed of the hostile conduct of Russia and Austria, the emperor said:

> I am about to quit my capital to place myself at the head of my army in order that I may render prompt assistance to my allies, and defend the dearest interests of my people . . . I groan for the blood which it will cost Europe; but it will be the means of adding new lustre to the French name.

Another campaign against the kings of Europe was inevitable, and he proceeded to achieve the destruction of Mack's army, not as at Marengo by one general battle, but by a series of grand manoeuvres, and a train of partial actions necessary to execute them, which rendered assistance and retreat alike impossible.

The great army that had been assembled on the coast of France to invade England was now relieved from its inactivity and directed to march upon the German frontiers. The Count de Ségur, who had command of the detachment of the Guard at the Tuileries, and accompanied Napoleon on this campaign, relates in his *Memoirs* a remarkable scene in the emperor's private quarters at Boulogne before Napoleon started for the frontier. The emperor had just received news that Admiral Villeneuve had taken the French fleet to Ferrol and left the channel. On learning this the emperor at once decided that the contemplated invasion of England was then impossible. Ségur then says:

> 'Sit there,' Napoleon said to M. Daru, then acting as intendant-general of the army 'and write.' And then, without a transition, without any apparent meditation, with his brief and imperious accent, he dictated to him, without hesitation, the plan of the campaign of Ulm as far as Vienna! The army of the coast, fronting the ocean for more than two hundred leagues, was at the first signal to turn round and march on the Danube, in several columns! The order of the marches, their duration, points of concentration, of reunion of the columns, surprises, attacks, various movements, the enemy's mistakes—all was foreseen . . . The battlefields, the victories, even the dates on which we were to enter Munich and Vienna—all was then written just as it happened, and this two months in advance, at this very hour of the 13th of August, and from this quarter-general on the coast. Daru, however accustomed to the inspirations of his chief, remained dumfounded, and he was even more surprised when afterwards he saw these oracles realised.

The emperor returned to Paris without delay, and there laid before the Senate the state of the army and announced the commencement of hostilities.

It was five years since the soldiers had been in battle; and for two and a half years they had been waiting in vain for an opportunity to cross over into England. It would be difficult to form any conception then of their joy or of their ardour when they learned they were going to be employed in a great war. Old and young ardently longed for battles, dangers, distant expeditions. They had conquered the Austrians, the Prussians, the Russians; they despised all the soldiers of Europe and did not imagine there was an army in the world capable of resisting them. They set off singing, and shouting, "*Vive l'Empereur!*"

At the same time Massena received orders to assume the offensive in Italy, and force his way, if possible, into the hereditary States of Austria. The two French armies, one crossing the Rhine and the other pushing through the Tyrolese, looked forward to a junction before the walls of Vienna. After appointing Joseph Bonaparte to superintend the government in his absence Napoleon quitted Paris on the 24th of September 1805, accompanied as far as Strasburg by Josephine: here they separated. The emperor put himself at the head of his army and crossed the Rhine on the 1st of October. He now begun a series of grand manoeuvres and partial actions, requiring consummate skill, with a view to the destruction of the great Austrian Army under General Mack.

Mack, at the head of the Austrian forces, established his headquarters on the western frontier of Bavaria, at Ulm. Prudence would have suggested that he occupy the line of the River Inn, which, extending from the Tyrol to the Danube at Passau, affords a strong defence to the Austrian territory, and on which he might have awaited, in comparative safety, the arrival of the Russian forces, then on the march to aid Austria in the campaign.

Napoleon hastened to profit by Mack's error, and by a combination of manoeuvres with his different divisions, the great body of the French Army advanced into the heart of Germany by the left of the Danube, and then throwing himself across the river, took ground in the Austrian general's rear, when he expected to be assaulted in front of Ulm. As it was, Mack's communication with Vienna was interrupted, and he was completely isolated.

Never was astonishment equal to that which filled all Europe on the unexpected arrival of the French Army. It was supposed to be on the shores of the ocean, and in twenty days, scarcely time enough for the report of its march to spread to this point, it appeared on the Rhine.

Napoleon did not effect his purpose of taking up a position in the rear of Mack without resistance, but in the various engagements with the different divisions of the Austrian Army at Wertingen, Gunzburgh, Memingen and Elchingen, the French were uniformly successful. At Memingen General Spangenburg was forced to capitulate, and 5,000 men laid down their arms. Not less than 20,000 prisoners fell into the hands of the French between the 26th of September and the 13th of October.

The emperor passed in review the dragoons of the village of Zumershausen when he ordered to be brought before him a dragoon named Marente, of the 4th regiment, one of the gallant soldiers who, at the passage of the Lech, had saved his captain, by whom he had, a few days before, been cashiered from his rank. Napoleon then bestowed upon him the eagle of the Legion of Honour.

The soldier observed:

> I have only done my duty, my captain degraded me on account of some violation of discipline but he knows I have always proved a good soldier.

The emperor expressed his satisfaction to the dragoons for the bravery they had displayed at the Battle of Wertingen and ordered each regiment to present a dragoon, on whom he also bestowed the decoration of the Legion of Honour.

Napoleon looked upon the Battle of Elchingen which followed the actions at Wertingen and Gunzburgh as one of the finest feats of arms that his army had ever accomplished. From this field of battle, he sent the Senate forty standards taken by the French Army in the various battles which had succeeded that of Wertingen. He wrote:

Since my entry on this campaign, I have disposed of an army of 100,000 men. I have taken nearly half of them prisoners; the rest have either deserted, are killed, wounded, or reduced to the greatest consternation. Assisted by Divine Providence I hope in a short time to triumph over all my enemies.

By the 13th of October General Mack found himself completely surrounded at Ulm with a garrison of fully 20,000 good troops. On this day Napoleon made an exciting address to his soldiers on the bridge of the Lech, amid the most intense cold, the ground being covered with snow, and the troops sunk to the knees in mud. He warned them to expect a great battle, and explained the desperate condition of the enemy. He was answered with acclamations and repeated shouts of, "*Vive l'Empereur!*" In listening to his exciting words, the soldiers forgot their fatigues and privations and were impatient to rush into the fight.

As Napoleon passed through a crowd of prisoners, an Austrian colonel expressed his astonishment on beholding the Emperor of the French drenched with rain, covered with dirt, and as much, or even more fatigued than the meanest drummer in his army. An *aide-de-camp* present having explained to him what the Austrian officer said, the emperor ordered this answer to be given:

> Your master wished me to recollect that I was a soldier; I hope that he will allow that the throne and the Imperial purple have not made me forget my original profession.

From the height of the Abbey of Elchingen Napoleon now beheld the city of Ulm at his feet, commanded on every side by his cannon; his victorious troops ready for the assault, and the great Austrian Army cooped up within the walls. Four days later a flag of truce came from General Mack.

Napoleon had called upon the commander to surrender, and unlike the brave Wurmser, who held Mantua to extremity during the campaign of Alvinzi, he capitulated without hazarding a blow. On the previous day Mack had published a proclamation urging his troops to prepare for the "utmost pertinacity of de-

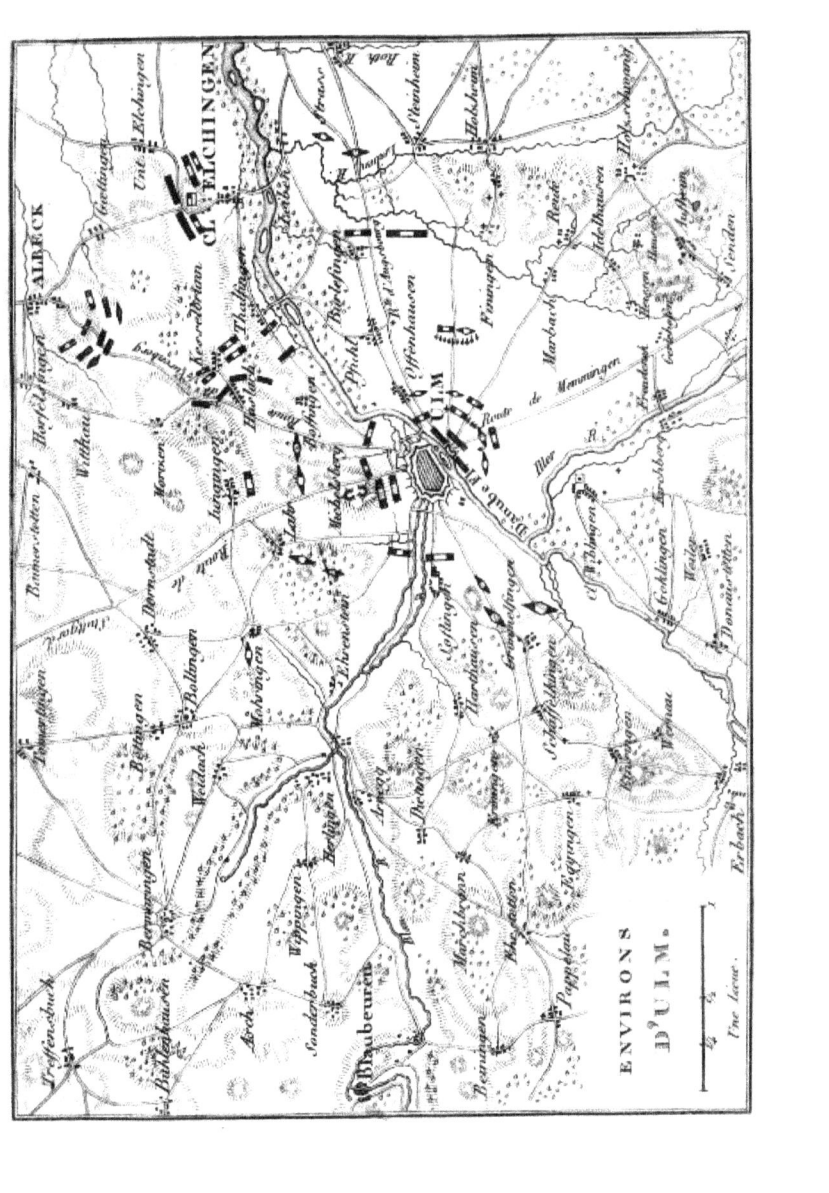

fence" and forbidding, on the pain of death, the very word "surrender" to be breathed within the walls of Ulm. He announced the arrival of two powerful armies, one of Austrians, the other of Russians, whose appearance "would presently raise the blockade." He even declared his intention of eating horseflesh rather than listen to any terms of capitulation!

On the morning of October 15th Napoleon finally resolved to bring the affair to a close, and gave orders to Marshal Ney to storm the heights of Michaelsberg. All at once a battery unmasked by the Austrians, poured its grapeshot upon the Imperial group. Lannes, who was to flank Ney, abruptly seized Napoleon's horse to lead him out of the galling fire. The latter had taken up a position to watch Ney, who had set his columns in motion. Changing to a safe position, the emperor saw this intrepid leader climb the intrenchments raised on Michaelsberg, and carry them with the bayonet. Lannes secured another point of attack a moment later.

Napoleon then suspended the combat until the next day, when he ordered a few shells to be thrown into Ulm, and in the evening sent Ségur to General Mack summoning him to surrender. The envoy had great difficulty in getting into the place. He was led blindfold before Mack, who, striving to conceal his anxiety, was nevertheless unable to dissemble his surprise and grief on learning the extent of his disaster and hopeless position.

On the 17th Mack signed articles by which hostilities were immediately ceased and he with all his men agreed to surrender (!) themselves as prisoners of war within ten days, unless some Austrian or Russian force should appear and attempt to raise the blockade. On the 19th, after a personal visit to Napoleon's camp, Mack submitted to a "revision" of the treaty, and on the 20th a formal evacuation of Ulm took place.

Thirty-six thousand soldiers filed off and laid down their arms before Napoleon and his staff. A large watchfire had been made, near which the emperor posted himself to witness the ceremony. General Mack came forward and delivered his sword, exclaiming, with grief: "Here is the unfortunate Mack!" Napoleon received him and his officers with the greatest courtesy. Eighteen generals

Capitulation of Ulm

were dismissed on parole, an immense quantity of ammunition of all sorts fell into the hands of the victor, and a wagonful of Austrian standards was sent to Paris.

Napoleon enforced the strictest silence on his troops while this ceremony, so painful to their enemies continued. In one instance he instantly ordered out of his presence one of his own generals from whom his quick ear caught some witticism passed on the occasion.

All the Austrian officers were allowed to return home, on giving their word of honour not to serve against France until a general exchange of prisoners should take place.

This campaign is perhaps unexampled in the history of warfare for the greatness of its results in comparison with the smallness of the expense at which they were obtained. Of the French Army, scarcely fifteen hundred men were killed and wounded; while the Austrian Army of almost ninety thousand men was nearly annihilated; all, with the exception of 15,000 who escaped, being killed, wounded, or prisoners; and having lost also, 200 pieces of cannon and ninety flags. It was a common remark among the troops:

> The emperor has found a new method of carrying on war; he makes us use our legs instead of our bayonets.

Five-sixths of the French Army never fired a shot, at which the troops were much mortified!

Massena was also successful in his advance from Lombardy, the Archduke Charles, who commanded an army of 80,000 men for Austria, being forced to abandon Italy, and Marshal Ney whom Napoleon had detached from his own main army with orders to advance in the Tyrol, was no less successful. The number of prisoners taken in this campaign was so great that Napoleon distributed them amongst the agriculturists that their work in the fields might make up for the absence of the conscripts, whom he had withdrawn from such labour.

Rumours of the approach of the Russians, headed by the emperor Alexander in person, came fast and frequent. The divisions of Massena and Ney were now at the disposal of Napoleon, who was concentrating his forces for the purpose of attacking Vienna, and, with the main body, now moved on the capital of the Austrian Emperor. The emperor Francis, perceiving that Vienna was incapable of defence, quitted his palace on the 7th of November, and proceeded to the headquarters of Alexander at Brünn.

While Napoleon was riding on horseback on the Vienna Road, he perceived an open carriage approaching, in which were seated a priest, and a lady bathed in tears. The emperor was dressed, as usual, in the uniform of a colonel of the *chasseurs* of the guard. The lady did not recognise him. He inquired the cause of her distress and where she was going.

"Sir," said she, "I have been robbed, about two leagues hence, by a party of soldiers, who have killed my gardener. I am going to request that your emperor will grant me a guard; he once knew my family well, and lay under obligations to them,"

"Your name?" inquired Napoleon,

"De Brünny" answered the lady. "I am the daughter of M. de Marbeuf, formerly Governor of Corsica."

"I am delighted to meet with you *madame*," exclaimed Napoleon with the most charming frankness, "and to have an opportunity of serving you—I am the emperor."

The lady expressed much surprise and passed on agreeing to wait for the commander at headquarters. Here she was furnished a piquet of *chasseurs*.

On the 13th the French entered Vienna, and Napoleon took up his residence in the Imperial Palace of SchoenBrünn, the home of the Austrian Caesars. While at this point Napoleon learned of the success of the English at Trafalgar on October 19th—the day after Mack surrendered at Ulm. It was a battle sternly contested and resulted in the final annihilation of the French fleet. Great as the triumph was for England, it was dearly purchased—for Nelson fell, mortally wounded, early in the action. He lived just long enough to hear the cheers of victory, and as he passed away, said, "Thank God! I have done my duty!"

The tidings of Trafalgar served but as a new stimulus to Napoleon's energy, he said:

Heaven has given the Empire of the Sea to England, but

Battle of Trafalgar

to us has fate decreed the dominion of the land.

But though such signal success had crowned the commencement of the campaign, it was necessary to defeat the haughty Russians before the object of the war could be considered as attained. The broken and shattered remnant of the Austrian forces had rallied from different quarters around the yet untouched army of Alexander; Napoleon had therefore waited until the result of his skilful combinations had drawn around him the greatest force he could expect to collect, ere venturing upon a general battle. He then quitted Vienna and put himself at the head of his columns which soon found themselves within reach of the Russian and Austrian forces, at length combined and ready for action, and under the eye of their emperors.

Now it was to be a battle of three emperors—France, Russia and Austria. Napoleon fixed his headquarters at Brünn, where he arrived on the 20th of November, and riding over the plain between this point and Austerlitz, a village about two miles from Brünn, said to his generals: "Study this field well—we shall, ere long, have to contest it."

Napoleon, on learning that the Emperor Alexander was personally in the hostile camp, sent Savary to present his compliments to that sovereign, and of course "incidentally to observe as much as he could of the numbers and condition of the enemy's troops." The messenger reported that the Russians laboured under a belief that the reverses of the previous campaign were the result of unpardonable cowardice among the Austrians, and the first general battle would show the sort of warriors the Russians were. Savary said that from the conversations he had for three days with nearly thirty coxcombs about the person of Alexander, that presumption, inconsiderateness, and imprudence, reigned in the decisions of the military as much as in the political cabinet, and that an army so conducted must of necessity commit great faults.

The *Czar* sent a young *aide-de-camp* to return the compliment carried by Savary, and he found the French soldiery engaged in fortifying their position—a position which Napoleon had some time before determined to occupy; but the negotiations were of no avail: Napoleon wanted either an overwhelming battle or peace. The *aide-de-camp* sent by Alexander was impressed with what appeared to him to be evidence of fear and apprehension on the part of the French. The placing of strong guards and fortifications, thrown up with such haste, appeared to him like the precautions of an army half beaten. The Russian prince discussed every point with an air of impertinence difficult to be conceived. He spoke to Napoleon as if he had been conversing with a Russian officer; but the emperor repressed his indignation, and the young man returned under a full conviction that the French Army was on the brink of ruin.

Several old Austrian generals, who had made campaigns against Napoleon, are said to have warned the Russian council against too much confidence as they were to march against old soldiers and able officers. They said they had seen Napoleon, when reduced to a handful of men, repossess himself of victory, under the most difficult circumstances, by rapid and unforeseen operations, in which manner he had destroyed numerous armies. The presumptuous young man declared that the presence of the Russian Emperor would inspire the troops to victory especially as they would be aided by the picked troops of the Imperial Guard of Russia.

On the 1st of December, on seeing the Russians begin to descend from a chain of heights on which they might have received an attack with great advantage to themselves, and have remained in safety until the Archduke Charles could come up with the 80,000 men in Bohemia and Hungary, Napoleon exclaimed rapturously, as he witnessed the rash manoeuvre:

> In twenty-four hours that army will be mine!

In the meantime, withdrawing his outposts and concentrating his forces, he continued to imitate a conscious inferiority, which was far from existing. In the order of the day (December 1) before the Battle of Austerlitz, Napoleon inserted the following proclamation:

> Soldiers, the Russians are before you, to avenge the Austrian army at Ulm. They consist of the same battalions you

Czar's Guard capture 4th Line regiment's standard at Austerlitz

beat at Hollenbrun and have constantly pursued. The positions we occupy are formidable; and, while they march to my right, they shall present me their flank.—Soldiers, I will direct myself all your battalions. I shall keep at a distance from the firing, if, with your accustomed bravery, you carry confusion and disorder into the enemy's ranks; but, should victory appear for a moment doubtful, you shall see your emperor expose himself to the first blows; for victory cannot hesitate on this day, in which the honour of the French infantry, of so much importance to the whole army, is concerned. Suffer not the ranks to be thinned, under pretence of carrying off the wounded; but let each man be well persuaded that we must conquer the hirelings of England, who are animated with so deep a hatred of our nation. This victory must terminate our campaign; when we shall resume our winter quarters, and be joined by the new armies forming in France. The peace which I make will be worthy of my people, of you and myself.

          (Signed)   Napoleon.

At one o'clock on the morning of the 2nd of December, Napoleon, having slept for an hour by a watchfire, got on horseback and proceeded to reconnoitre the front of his position. He wished to do so without being recognised, but the soldiers penetrated the secret, and, lighting great fires of straw along the line, 80,000 men received him from post to post with great enthusiasm. They reminded him that it was the anniversary of his coronation, and declared that they would celebrate the day in a manner worthy of his glory. One old grenadier cried:

> Only promise us, that you will keep yourself out of the fire: I promise you in the name of the grenadiers of the army that you will have to fight only with your eyes, and we will bring you the flags and artillery of the Russian Army to celebrate the anniversary of your coronation.

The emperor answered:

I will do so, but I shall be with the reserve *until you need us.*

This promise Napoleon soon repeated in his proclamation. As he threw down his pen after signing this document, he exclaimed:

> This is the noblest evening of my life; but I shall lose too many of these brave fellows tomorrow. The anguish which I experience at this idea makes me feel they are really my children; and truly I am vexed with myself for these sensations, as I fear they will unman me on the field of battle.

In his preparations for this decisive contest which he made immediately, ten battalions of the Imperial Guard, with ten of Oudinot's division, were to be kept in reserve in the rear of the line, under the eyes of Napoleon himself, who destined them, with forty field-pieces, to act wherever the fate of battle should render their services most necessary.

Ségur says:

> The battle was planned by Napoleon in every detail, just as he had planned the strategic movements of the army. In the early morning he sent for all his *aides-de-camp* to come to the small house where he had spent the night. We had a slight repast, which, like himself, we ate standing; after which, putting on his sword, he said, 'Now gentlemen, let us go and begin a great day.' We all ran to our horses. A moment afterwards we saw, on the top of the hill which the soldiers called 'the Emperor's hill,' arriving from the various points of our line, followed each by their *aides-de-camp*, all the chiefs of our army corps, Murat, Lannes, Bernadotte, Soult, Davoust—all coming to receive final orders. If I were to live as long as the world shall last, I would never forget that scene.

After a hazy, misty daybreak, the sun at last arose with uncommon brilliancy, so bright in fact that "the sun of Austerlitz" afterwards fell into a proverb with the French soldiery, who hailed similar dawns with exultation and as a sure omen of victory. The emperor said, as he passed in front of several regiments:

French right flank

Soldiers, we must finish this campaign by a thunderbolt which shall confound the pride of our enemies.

Immediately they raised their hats on the bayonets' points and cries of, "Live the Emperor!" formed the actual signal for battle. A moment afterwards the horizon cleared up and as the sun darted forth its glistening rays the cannonading was heard at the extremity of the right line. The great Battle of Austerlitz had begun.

At the opening of the engagement, Kutusoff, the Russian general-in-chief, fell into a snare laid for him by Napoleon, and sent a large division of his army to turn the right of the French. His troops, detached tor this purpose, met with unexpected resistance from Davoust, and were held in check. Napoleon at once seized the opportunity given him by the enemy in leaving a deep gap in their line, and upon that space Soult forthwith poured a force which entirely cut oil all communication between the Russian centre and left.

The *Czar* quickly perceived the fatal consequences of the movement, and ordered his guards to rush to the eminence called the hill of Pratzen, where the encounter was taking place, and beat back Soult. The Russians succeeded in driving the French before them, when Napoleon ordered Bessières to their rescue with the Imperial Guards. The Russians had become somewhat disordered from the impatience of their temporary victory, and although they resisted Bessières sternly, they were finally broken and fled. The regiment of the Grand Duke Constantine, who gallantly led the Russians, was now annihilated and the duke only escaped by the fleetness of his horse.

The French centre now advanced, and the charges of Murat's cavalry were most decisive, while the left wing, under the command of Lannes, marched forward, *en echelons*, by regiments, in the same manner as if they had been exercising by divisions. A tremendous cannonade then took place along the whole line; two hundred and three pieces of cannon, and nearly two hundred thousand men, being engaged, so that it was indeed a giant combat. Success could not be doubtful: in a moment the Russians were all but routed, their colonel, artillery, standards and

RUSSIAN UNIFORMS, 1805

everything being already captured. At 1 o'clock the victory was decided; it had never been doubtful for a moment; and not a man of the reserves was required.

From the heights of Austerlitz, the Emperors of Russia and Austria beheld the total ruin of their centre as they had already of their left. The right wing only remained unbroken, it having contested well the impetuous charge of Lannes; but Napoleon could now gather round them on all sides, and, his artillery plunging incessant fire on them from the heights, they at length found it impossible to hold their ground and were driven from position to position. They were at last forced down into a hollow where some frozen lakes offered them the only means of escape from the closing cannonade. As they did so the French broke the ice about them by a storm of shot from 200 heavy cannon, and nearly 2,000 men died on the spot, some swept away by artillery, but the greater part being drowned beneath the broken ice.

The cries of the dying Russians, as they sank beneath the waters, were drowned, however, by the victorious shouts of the French, who were pursuing the scattering remnants of the enemy in every direction. In the bulletin of the engagement Napoleon compared the scene to that at Aboukir, "when the sea was covered with turbans."

The emperor had addressed his soldiers on the evening preceding the battle to heighten their courage, and presage to them the victory; he did not forget to address himself to them again after the fight, and felicitate them upon having so nobly contributed to verify his prediction. He said to them:

> Soldiers, You have on this day of Austerlitz justified all that which I expected from your intrepidity. You have decorated your eagles with immortal glory. When all that is necessary to assure the happiness and prosperity of our country is accomplished, I will lead you back to France. There you will be the objects of my tenderest solicitude. My people will joyously greet you again, and it will suffice for you to say: 'I was at the Battle of Austerlitz,' and for them to reply, 'Behold a brave man!'

In later years Napoleon said of this engagement:

> I have fought thirty battles like that, but I have never seen so decisive a victory, or one where the chances were so unevenly balanced.

At another time while at St. Helena he said:

> If I had not conquered at Austerlitz I should have had all Prussia on me.

It was with great difficulty that the Emperors of Russia and Austria rallied some fragments of their armies around them, and, terror-stricken, effected their retreat. With the conqueror there remained 20,000 prisoners, 40 pieces of artillery, and all the standards of the Imperial Guard of Russia. Such was the Battle of Austerlitz, or as the French soldiers delighted to call it, "The Battle of the Emperors"; and thus did Napoleon's army fulfil its pledge to celebrate the anniversary of his coronation.

The fleeing emperors halted at midnight for council, and decided to send a messenger to Napoleon at daylight with proposals for peace. The envoy was courteously received, and arrangements were at once made for a meeting of the Austrian and French emperors at ten o'clock the next day. They met about three leagues from Austerlitz, near a mill. Napoleon was the first to arrive on the ground; he at once ordered that two fires be made, and with a squadron of his Guard drawn up at a distance of about two hundred paces, awaited the arrival of Francis and his personal suite.

When Francis came in sight, accompanied by several princes and generals, and an escort of Hungarian cavalry, Napoleon advanced to his carriage, and embraced him. The two emperors, each with an attendant, then went to one of the fires near the entrance to a military hut, while the suites of the two sovereigns drew around the other fire, a few paces distant.

"Such are the palaces you have compelled me to occupy for these three months," said Napoleon, pointing to his modest quarters.

"You have made such good use of them," answered Francis,

"that you ought not to complain of their accommodation."

The defeated emperor is represented as having thrown the blame of the war upon the English. "They are a set of merchants," he said, "who would set the continent on fire, in order to secure themselves the commerce of the world."

When the two great leaders separated, after an interview lasting an hour, they again embraced. Napoleon saying in the hearing of the gentlemen of the suites—Prince John of Lichtenstein, near Francis, and Marshal Berthier, near Napoleon—:"I agree to it; but Your Majesty must not make war upon me again."

"No, I promise you I will not," said Francis in reply; "I will keep my word"—a promise that was soon violated.

It was understood that the Emperor of Russia, although not present, was to abide by the agreement for an armistice. Alexander so assured Marshal Davoust, who had pursued him the night of the battle, and the Russians were allowed by Napoleon to retire unmolested to their own territory, on the royal word of Francis that Russia would adhere to his ally of Austria.

Napoleon said to Francis:

> The Russian Army is surrounded. Not a man can escape me but I wish to oblige their emperor, and will stop the march of my columns if Your Majesty promises me that these Russians shall evacuate Germany, and the Austrian and Prussian parts of Poland.

"It is the purpose of the Emperor Alexander to do so," was the reply. No other engagement was required of the *Czar* than his word.

When the negotiations had been completed, and the Emperor Francis had departed, Napoleon walked hurriedly to and fro for a short time, and after a deep silence he was heard to say:

> I have acted very unwisely. I could have followed up my victory, and taken up the whole of the Austrian and Russian Armies. They are both entirely in my power. But—let it be. It will at least cause some less tears to be shed.

Napoleon then went over the field of battle, ordering the

wounded to be removed, when some of those unfortunates, forgetting their sufferings asked, "Is the victory quite certain?"

The foot guards of the emperor, not having been permitted to engage, actually wept and insisted upon doing something to identify them with the victory

"Be satisfied," said Napoleon, "you are the reserve; it will be better if you have nothing to do today."

The commander of the artillery of the Imperial Russian Guard having lost his cannon, met the French emperor and said, "Sire, order me to be shot, I have lost my cannon."

"Young man," replied Napoleon, "I esteem your grief; but one may be beaten by my army, and still retain some pretension to glory."

The brief campaign was followed by a treaty with the Emperor of Austria, signed December 15th, 1805, and another with Prussia, signed December 26th at Vienna. The victor of Austerlitz made his own terms in the negotiations. Austria gave up the last of her Italian usurpations to be annexed to the Kingdom of Italy, and the Tyrol to Bavaria, and yielded other stipulations which the conqueror demanded, but which were so moderate that they excited the wonder and admiration of all Europe.

Previous to Napoleon's departure for SchoenBrünn on the 27th of December he issued the following proclamation to his army:

> Soldiers! Peace between myself and the Emperor of Austria is signed. You have, in this late season of the year, made two campaigns. You have performed everything I expected. I am setting out for my capital. I have promoted and distributed rewards to those who have most distinguished themselves. I will perform everything I have promised. You have seen that Your Emperor has shared all your dangers and fatigues; you shall likewise behold him surrounded by all that grandeur and splendour which become the sovereign of the first nation in the world. In the beginning of the month of May, I will give a grand festival in Paris; you shall all be there. We will celebrate the memory of those who, in these campaigns have fallen on the field of hon-

our. The world shall see that we are ready to follow their example, and, if necessary, do more than we have done, against those who suffer themselves to be misled by the gold of the eternal enemy of the continent.

The news of the success of the army was received with the greatest enthusiasm by the majority of the French people.

Madame de Remusat in writing to her husband from Paris after the receipt of the news of the Battle of Austerlitz, said:

You cannot imagine how excited everyone is. Praise of the Emperor is on everyone's lips; The most recalcitrant are obliged to lay down their arms, and to say with the Emperor of Russia, 'He is a man of destiny.'

The campaign had consolidated the empire of Napoleon, and when he returned to France he was received with exultation by the citizens, who tendered him *fête* after *fête* such as had not been witnessed at the capital for years. This was followed by the elevation of many of his kinsmen and heroes to thrones of pomp and power, coronation following coronation in rapid succession, princedoms and dukedoms being accompanied with grants of extensive estates in the countries which the French Armies had conquered. From that moment, the fanaticism of military glory quite effaced the few remaining impressions made by the love of liberty.

A Synopsis of the Austerlitz Campaign
J. H. Henderson

The March on Ulm

On August 25 the seven Corps of the Grand Army were put in motion towards the Rhine and the Main: I. Corps (Bernadotte), from Hanover on Wurzburg to unite with the Bavarian Corps; II. Corps (Marmont), from Holland on Mayence and thence on Wurzburg; III. Corps (Davout), IV. Corps (Soult), VI. Corps (Ney), V. Corps (Lannes), from the camp of Boulogne on Mannheim, Spire, Carlsruhe, Strasburg; VII. Corps (Augereau), from Brest on Strasburg, to act as a Reserve, together with the Imperial Guard (Bessières).

On the same place also were to move 22,000 Cavalry under Murat. By September 25 these movements were completed with remarkable precision. To deceive the Austrians as to the true line of operations, Napoleon feinted with cavalry from Strasburg through the Black Forest, whilst his columns poured on to the Danube at Donauwerth, October 6, cutting Mack's line with Vienna. The French troops then completely surrounded Ulm on both sides of the river, driving the enemy back on the fortress. Mack, paralysed by the danger and without supplies, capitulated October 20, with 33,000 men and 60 guns.

Operations in Italy.

Massena and the Archduke Charles watched each other on the Adige, waiting for the result of the German campaign. On the news of the French success there, Massena, on October 30, attacked the Austrian at Caldiero; the latter retired in the night towards Hungary *via* Laibach and Klagenfürt, followed by Massena, who, however, could not move far, because he and St. Cyr had to be ready to oppose the Anglo-Russians at Naples.

March on Vienna.

After Mack's surrender the emperor, spite of Prussia's threatening attitude and of the English victory at Trafalgar (October 21), moved on Vienna, intending to fight the Russians, who had 54,000 under Kutusof on the River Inn, and 30,000 under Buxhöwden in Moravia.

On the right, Ney and Augereau in the Tyrol captured Jellachich, and opposed the Archduke John, who, passing through the Brenner, managed to join the Archduke Charles in Carinthia, and both archdukes then retired towards the Raab in Hungary; in the right centre, Bernadotte and Marmont on Salzburg on the River Inn; in the centre, Napoleon, with Murat's cavalry and the corps of Soult, Davout, and Lannes, crossed the Rivers Inn, Traun, and Enns; on the left, down the north bank of the Danube, marched Mortier with three divisions, which a flotilla was to connect with the centre. The emperor caught up the rearguard of Kutusof; the latter, however, passed the Danube at Krems, burnt the bridge, and fell on Mortier (isolated and far ahead of his flotilla), inflicting a loss of 3,000 men.

Meantime, Murat dashed on Vienna, and by means of a feigned armistice seized the great bridge there. The emperor, on November 5, entered the Austrian capital.

Campaign of Moravia.

Master of Vienna and of its bridge, the French sovereign resolved to cut off Kutusof's retreat into Moravia. The Russian, intercepted, managed, by employing a stratagem similar to Murat's, to escape and to rally the Austro-Russian forces at Olmütz, commanded by the two Emperors, Francis and Alexander. Napoleon, on November 19, established his headquarters at Brünn. His pretended hesitation and his delusive negotiations induced the Allies to advance towards Austerlitz, where the French Monarch accepted battle.

Battle of Austerlitz, December 2.

The Austro-Russians, elated by a slight success at Wischau, decided on battle. The French, 68,000 strong, stood in front of Brünn, in the angle formed by the Vienna and Olmütz roads, and behind the Goldbach stream, along which extended the lakes of Kobelnitz, Sokolnitz, Satschan, and Mönitz. The Allies, 90,000 strong, had their headquarters at Austerlitz; their right—Bagration and the cavalry of Lichtenstein—on the Olmütz road, east of Bosenitz; their centre—Kutusof—near Pratzen; their left—Buxhöwden—on Aujezd; their Reserve (the Russian Imperial Guard) near Austerlitz.

Napoleon divined that they would try to turn his right, in order to cut him off from Vienna and to throw him back on Bohemia; as a fact he had an alternative line of retreat on Linz. He therefore allowed them to occupy (December 1) the plateau of Pratzen, an elevated region between the two Armies; and thus disposed his forces: on the left, Lannes and Murat near Bosenitz, backed on Santon and its batteries, were to contain the enemy's right; on the right, Legrand with 7,000 men along the Goldbach from Kobelnitz to Telnitz, was to hold the Russian left, this small force of 7,000 would be reinforced early on December 2 by 8,000 under Davout from Gross Raigern; in the centre stood a powerful mass of 50,000 — Soult on the Goldsbach between Girzikowitz and Kobelnitz, having for his objective the plateau of Pratzen, behind him Bernadotte, and in Reserve, near Schlapanitz, the Grenadiers of Oudinot and the Imperial Guard.

The battle opened on the French right. Buxhöwden descended by Aujezd from the plateau and succeeded in crossing the Goldbach and in driving Legrand out of Telnitz and Sokolnitz. At that moment Davout appeared, and regaining Sokolnitz, managed to hold the hostile masses pouring down from the plateau. It was exactly what Napoleon desired. On the French left Bagration attempted to outflank, but Lannes having repulsed him delivered, with Murat's help, a counter-stroke which, in spite of Lichtenstein's charges, ended; in the Allies retiring along the Olmütz road. In the French centre, Napoleon, seeing the plateau almost deserted, the hostile left occupied with Davout,

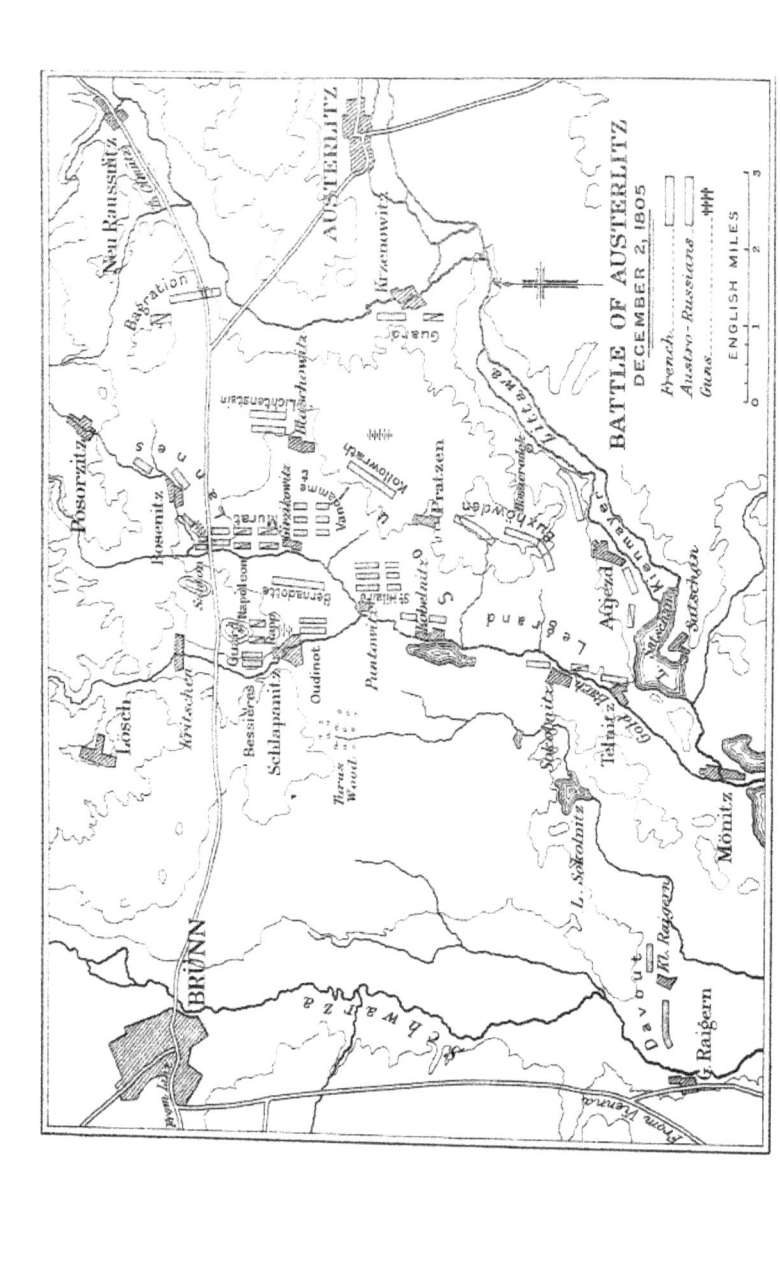

and their right repulsed, launched Soult on to the plateau. The two Divisions of Vandamme and Saint Hilaire, supported by Bernadotte, climbed up the slopes, without replying to the Russian fire, deployed and threw the enemy back upon the opposite slopes. Kutusof saw the danger. It was imperative to recapture the plateau. A counter-attack was made by the Russian Reserve (10,000 guard troops) and all other disposable bodies, but Napoleon had foreseen this, and called up his Reserve (25,000), who broke the enemy; the cavalry of Bessières, under Rapp, pushing as far as Austerlitz, cut the hostile forces in two.

Leaving Bernadotte to hold the plateau, the emperor swung Soult's corps to the right through Aujezd, thus bringing that marshal on the rear of Buxhöwden who was held in front by Davout. The former assailed on all sides tried to flee across the frozen lakes. The French cannon broke the ice, and men, horses, and cannon were engulphed. A vigorous pursuit was at once organised—Lannes and Murat towards Olmütz, Davout towards Hungary. Loss: Allies, 35,000 and 180 guns; French, 8,000.

Tactical Comments: (1) Errors of Allies were weakness of centre, bad reconnoitring, tardiness of the Reserve; they should not have fought at all, they should have retired, the Archduke Charles was moving towards the French right, Prussia was ready to descend on the French left; (2) It was on Napoleon's part a defensive-offensive battle; (3) The pursuit was vigorous; (4) Lannes' infantry combined skilfully with Murat's cavalry; (5) Soult's movements were perfect; (6) Napoleon induced the Allies to act as he desired.

The campaign closed with the Treaty of Pressburg, by which Austria gave up Venetia, Istria, Dalmatia to the Kingdom of Italy (formed from the Cisalpine Republic), the Tyrol and Austrian Swabia to Bavaria and Würtemberg, whose rulers became kings. Next the Treaty of Schönbrünn compelled Prussia to accept Hanover—Napoleon intending thus to sow discord between Prussia and England—assigned Cleves to France, Anspach to Bavaria. On July 12, 1806, was formed, under French protection, the Confederation of the Rhine—Baden, Bavaria, Würtemberg, several smaller states, and finally Saxony—and in the same year the Holy Roman Empire was dissolved, Francis becoming Emperor of Austria.

Strategic Comments: (1) The French soldiers remarked: "*L'Empereur a battu l'ennemi avec nos jambes*"; (2) This campaign is singularly like that of Marengo 1800; (3) In this campaign Napoleon first constituted *Corps d'Armée*, an Artillery Reserve, and a Cavalry Reserve; (4) His troops lived on the country, carrying four days' bread and four days' biscuit; (5) The visible telegraph was much used; (6) The Aulic Council committed three errors—100,000 men were left inactive in Italy, 80,000 only operated in Germany, 20,000 were wasted in the Tyrol.

THE GRAND ARMY OF FRANCE.

1st Corps under Bernadotte.
2nd   "   "   Marmont.
3rd   "   "   Davout.
4th   "   "   Soult (divisions of Vandamme, St. Hilaire, and Legrand).
5th   "   "   Cannes.
6th   "   "   Ney.
7th   "   "   Augereau.
Guard under Bessières.
Cavalry under Murat.

Lejeune's Experiences at Austerlitz

Louis-François Lejeune

I was working away at painting when I was summoned to follow Marshal Berthier to the camp of Boulogne in the capacity of an orderly officer.

Everyone knows how Napoleon, when he heard that war with him had been declared by the Austrians through the invasion by them of the territory of our allies the Bavarians, led the army from the camp at Boulogne to the shores of the Danube.

As for me, I had already taken a considerable share in all the eager sending to and fro of despatches, the embarkations, the manoeuvres of troops, &c., and I had ordered my post-horses to follow the Imperial staff to Alsace, when Marshal Berthier gave me orders from the emperor not to leave Boulogne till I had sent off by the quickest route for Germany 300,000 pairs of shoes to be delivered to me for the military stores. At the words *remain* and *shoes* I felt stupefied, and fell into utter despair. What had been the good of all my study, I said to myself, if I was to become a mere escort of shoes? Still, I put my whole heart into the matter, but the difficulties were very great, and I was not able to rejoin the emperor until October 14, 1805, whilst the Battle of Elchingen was going on.

In giving the emperor an account of my mission, and saying to him, 'The shoes are there,' I could not help grumbling at his having reduced me to the position of a mere army contractor, and deprived me of the honour of being present at the beginning of the campaign, to which he replied with a smile:

BARON LOUIS-FRANÇOIS LEJEUNE

What a child you are! You don't seem to understand the importance of the service you have just rendered; shoes help on marches, and marches win battles; you will get your turn as well as everyone else.

A day or two later, October 17, 1805, General Mack signed the capitulation of Ulm. It was a fine sight to see all the splendid Austrian and Hungarian regiments file by in their full-dress uniforms, all looking as fresh as possible still, for it was but eight days since the campaign began. The French Army was drawn up in divisions opposite the town and facing the heights of the Michael Berg, which rises like an amphitheatre behind it and looks down upon the left bank of the Danube, where the Austrians were marching past. This was of course a glorious spectacle for us, but at the same time rather an affecting one, for we could not but remember that the fortunes of war are fluctuating.

The army resumed its march immediately afterwards. Marshal Murat, with an energy which did much to insure us the victory, driving the enemy before him. Accustomed to overcome every obstacle, he cared but little for the fate of those he came across. But everything was by no means *couleur de rose*; it was now November 4, 1805, it was cold, and ground and trees in the Amstetten forest were alike covered with masses of snow, which produced a very remarkable effect on those of us who came from the South of Europe and had never before realised how beautiful nature can be in the winter. In this particular instance everything was robed in the most gleaming attire; the silvery rime softening the rich colours of the decaying oak leaves and the sombre vegetation of the pines.

The frozen drapery, combined with the mist in which everything was more or less enveloped, gave a soft mysterious charm to the surrounding objects, producing a most beautiful picture. Lit up by the sunshine, thousands of long icicles, such as those which sometimes droop from our fountains and water wheels, hung like shining lustres from the trees. Never did ballroom shine with so many diamonds; the long branches of the oaks, pines, and other forest trees were weighed down by the masses of hoar frost, whilst the snow converted their summits into rounded roofs, forming beneath them grottoes resembling those of the Pyrenean mountains with their shining stalactites and graceful columns, I called the attention of Marshal Murat to the beauty of the scene as we rode rapidly beneath the frozen vaults, pursuing a rearguard of cavalry which was fleeing before us, and we were still admiring the *grandeur* of the northern scene when a break in the forest suddenly revealed a very unexpected sight of a totally different character.

Eight Austrian and Hungarian regiments drawn up in order of battle awaited us unmoved at the entrance to the defile. Murat had very few men with him, yet he had the audacity to attack them. It was now the enemy's turn to charge us, which they did with splendid gallantry, and it was very difficult for us, though we turned right about at once, to get back to the protection of the pass. The enemy overtook us, their ranks were mingled with our rearguard, our men were swept down, many were taken prisoners, and we ourselves were in danger of being captured. Murat's horse was killed under him, mine fell in the confused rush down the steep path, and I was flung off. I should have been crushed by the onrush before I could get out of the way if I had not flung myself under the shelter of two pieces of cannon which a young officer of artillery, fresh from college, had the presence of mind to place in position in the middle of the path.

The *mêlée* was truly terrible, and swords were already clashing above our heads, when the young officer, having with admirable *sang-froid* made sure that his guns were properly pointed, sprang between the two cannons, fuse in hand, and just as he was going to be cut down, in less time than it takes to tell, he fired. The grape shot, with which the two cannons were charged, swept down the whole of the head of the enemy's column, which, spread out as it was across the slope of the entrance to the forest, presented a wide surface.

Not one single shot of the double discharge missed its victim; the shock brought down on our heads the masses of snow in the trees, and as if by enchantment the squadrons of the enemy disappeared in a cloud of smoke and a storm of snow mixed with great death-dealing icicles, which, falling from a height of more than one hundred feet, crashed upon the helmets of the fugitives with a resounding noise.

A sudden panic seized the Austrians, and they took to flight. Murat saw his opportunity, returned to the charge, and gave chase to the enemy. In the end we halted eight leagues farther on on the road to Vienna. I regret that I cannot give the name of the young artillery officer to whom we owed our success. I had not time to ask him what it was, but I know that Murat intended to recommend him for promotion.

We soon reached Vienna, but we only halted there for a short time, and pressed on in our pursuit of the Austrians and Russians. They meanwhile had managed to get near to Olmütz, a fortress in a strong position on a lofty plateau. There, protected by the fort, the enemy halted, apparently with the intention of giving us battle. Napoleon, however, was far too clever to leave to the Austrians and Russians, who were altogether more than 120,000 strong, the advantages of so fine a position, especially as the French Army, owing to the number of garrisons left behind *en route* to secure the retention of the districts conquered, was now reduced to some 60,000 men.

The emperor therefore sent me to reconnoitre the country round Brünn, to which he meant to try and entice the Russians, and give them battle on ground where the advantage would be on the side of the French. Napoleon himself was determined to choose the position, and with this end in view he drew back his advanced guard for several miles towards the heights, which seemed fitted by nature to be the theatre of an event of such tremendous importance as the coming battle.

This feigned movement of retreat did not fail to restore confidence to the enemy; they resumed the offensive, followed us, and fell into the trap.

On December 1, 1805, we were drawn up awaiting the enemy's forces, which soon appeared and halted when they saw how well prepared we were to receive them.

On the morning of the same day, I was sent with an order from the major-general to Marshal Bernadotte, whom I found on the height called Sokolnitz at the foot of a cross on which was a life-sized figure of Christ painted red. The marshal had had a fire lighted, and was standing near as naked to the waist as the Christ, performing some wonderful gymnastic exercise with his arms. I asked him what in the world he was doing stripped like that in the bitter cold? and he replied, 'My dear fellow, I am bracing myself by taking an air bath.' Little did he think then, when he was trying to get used to the climate, that he would one day be king of a northern country.

The day of December 1 was passed on either side in preparations as for some grand *fête*, and an hour after the darkness fell, the two armies, their dispositions satisfactorily made, settled down to rest in profound silence, broken only by the sound of chatting round the bivouac fires, where the soldiers merrily talked over past successes or those which they counted on achieving in the future. I shared the bivouac of the staff of Marshal Berthier, and it was a very lively one, for one of our comrades, M. Longchamps, who had been detained in France, had only been able to join us that day, and during his journey he had composed some verses which very aptly hit off the rapidity of our march. The arrival of this merry companion, who brought letters from home for each of us, was the most charming episode of the day.

The letters from our families, the portraits, and in some cases the love letters brought by the friendly singer, the Tokay wine which we drank straight from the casks through straws, the crackling of the bivouac fire, with the presentiment of a victory on the morrow, combined to raise our spirits to the highest pitch. By degrees, however, one after the other fell asleep, the songs ceased, and we were all closely wrapped in our cloaks and stretched comfortably on a little straw beneath the twinkling stars, when we were aroused by shouts of joy and the glare of brilliant illuminations.

Whilst we had been sleeping, our general had been keeping watch and completing his preparations. His army was but half as strong as that of the enemy. His soldiers had hitherto always been victorious; but with so small a force to deploy in the vast plains on which we were encamped, it was of the utmost importance to him to know whether the confidence of the troops in their own superiority would again be sufficient to make up for their inferiority in numbers. It had therefore occurred to him to go on foot, accompanied by Marshal Berthier only, throughout the camp, and listen unnoticed to the chat of the soldiers round their fires.

By eleven o'clock he had already traversed a great distance, when he was recognised. The soldiers, surprised at finding him in the midst of them, and afraid that he might lose his way going back to his headquarters (which consisted merely of a fire near his carriage), hastened to break up the shelters they had made of branches and straw, to use them as torches to light their Emperor home. One bivouac after another took up the task, and in less than a quarter of an hour 60,000 torches lit up the camp, whilst passionate cries of '*Vive l'Empereur!*' resounded on every side. The shouts and the illumination alarmed the enemy, who, fearing a surprise, came from every side to reconnoitre our outposts and remained under arms all night. The emperor meanwhile, rendered happy and secure by the proofs of affection he had just received from his whole army, was able to sleep in peace and security.

Only those who know the difficulty of securing a little straw to sleep on in camp can appreciate the sacrifice made by the men in burning all their beds to light their general home. The Prince of Wales, it is said, once lit a hundred-pound note, and held it burning for five minutes, to enable his friend the Duke of Orleans to look for a *louis d'or* he had dropped when playing cards, but this lesson in dignity for the duke cannot as an example of unselfish devotion be compared with the action of our soldiers in thus proving their love and enthusiasm for their illustrious chief.

This memorable evening, this beautiful winter night was succeeded by the rising of the brilliant sun of Austerlitz.

The 2nd of December was the anniversary of the coronation of the emperor, and it was eight o'clock in the morning when the sun appeared above the horizon of Moravia as pure and radiant as in the brightest days of spring.

A light mist subdued the brilliancy of the scene, but we could distinctly make out the 120,000 bayonets gleaming in the sunshine as they slowly approached us, forming a crescent as vast as the horizon. This manoeuvre was intended to threaten our right wing, intervene between us and the town of Brünn, which was about four or five miles off, cut off our retreat towards Vienna, take us prisoners, and probably send us eventually to freeze to death in Siberia.

The right wing of the Russians advancing by the Olmütz road met the divisions under Suchet and Caffarelli, supported by a division of cuirassiers. The Russian general, thinking that the position would be a difficult one to attack, ordered his regiments to put their haversacks down on the ground where they stood, and when they were relieved of what he thought would be an embarrassing weight in the struggle, he gave the order to charge, saying to his men, 'You will get the French haversacks, they are full of gold!'

The attack was indeed a spirited one, but our cannon caused some little confusion. Our *cuirassiers* noticed this, and in spite of the terrible fire from the Russians they flung themselves upon the enemy, overthrowing more than 10,000 men and taking them prisoners. Ten thousand haversacks ranged in rows remained in our possession; but our booty, vast as it appeared, resolved itself into 10,000 little black boxes or rather triptych reliquaries, each containing an image of St. Christopher carrying the infant Saviour over the water, with an equal number of pieces of black bread containing a good deal more straw and bran than barley or wheat. Such was the sacred and simple baggage of the Russians!

On the right of this position the village of Pratzen was set on fire by the first balls from the Russian guns. The enemy was, however, defeated there also, driven back or taken prisoners. The Vandamme, Saint-Hilaire, and Legrand divisions occupied the centre opposite Austerlitz on the heights of Krecznowitz. The enemy made most strenuous efforts here, and the struggle was prolonged. Our troops suffered greatly, and were beginning to lose ground, when the emperor sent his own Guard and came in person to their support. The arrival of the Imperial Guard enabled us to resume the offensive.

A picked corps of the Russian cavalry was just charging when Colonel Morland at the head of the *élite* of the French Army flung himself upon them, overthrew them together with their artillery in the deep ravine of the Krecznowitz stream, pursuing them to the very foot of the castle of Austerlitz, the property of Prince Kaunitz. Colonel Morland was killed, and General Rapp wounded in the *mêlée*. I was in the thick of it too, and returned at the same time as the general to report to the emperor. The return was really more dangerous than the charge, for the enemy pelted us with shells. A *chasseur* of the Guard, who was already wounded, disappeared from my side with his horse, a shell having exploded inside the latter and blown both victims to pieces, leaving literally nothing but their shattered bones.

This brilliant struggle had taken place in the central division of our army, whilst the right was going through the most terrible experiences.

The enemy persevered with the greatest obstinacy in the attack, with a view to turning our right wing. A hot fusillade had been going on ever since eight in the morning, and the fortunes of the day fluctuated greatly opposite the villages of Tellnitz and Menitz. The emperor sent me to Marshal Davout, who was on our extreme right, with an order to push forward to the support of the centre. When I arrived, the marshal had already taken the initiative, and had been fighting for an hour in the village of Menitz. His troops had been three times repulsed, and three times he had driven out the Russians.

The wide Rue de Menitz, which was some four or five hundred yards long, was literally choked up with the dead and wounded of both armies, piled one on top of another, and it was all but impossible to ride over the heaps of mutilated bodies and weapons. Marshal Davout's infantry, however, managed to debouch from the village in spite of the resistance of the Russians, who were finally repulsed by the hot fire opened on them from the Saint-Hilaire and Legrand divisions, who pursued them for some distance.

On my way back to the emperor with M. de Sopranzy and

some twenty dragoons, we found ourselves compelled to pass through a Russian column. One of the generals in a very simple uniform with a few troopers tried to bar our passage, but we pushed right through them and wounded the general in the arm, whilst M. de Sopranzy seized the bridle of his horse and we dragged him along with us to our own ranks. I asked him his name, and he replied, 'I am the Baron de Wimpffen.'

He was in fact first cousin of Lieutenant-General Baron de Wimpffen, who held high rank in the French service, and was an intimate friend of my father's. The emperor, to whom we presented our prisoner, received him very courteously, and ordered his own surgeon, M. Yvan, to dress his wounds. Then, noticing that I was very much heated and bathed in sweat, he ordered a page in waiting to go and fetch me a glass of Bordeaux from his private canteen, which I drank with the toast, 'Success to the Emperor!'

This little scene took place on a high mound above the village of Augesd, opposite the lakes, or rather the big ponds, formed by the Tellnitz dyke. Meanwhile the Austro-Russian corps, driven back by Marshal Davout and unable to rejoin the main body at Austerlitz, were endeavouring to escape by way of the Tellnitz dyke, and thus to reach the road to Hungary; but the height was already occupied by the artillery of the Guard, and the cavalry alone ventured to risk the passage, galloping by under a hail of grape shot, whilst the infantry, hesitating what to do, finally imagined that their only chance of safety was to try and cross the ponds dividing them from the other side on the ice floating on their surfaces.

A few men, indeed, might have got over safely; but when a number had reached the middle of the water, the ice began to crack beneath their weight. They paused, and the troops behind them pushing on, there were soon some 6,000 men. collected in a dense crowd on the swaying slippery ice. There was a pause, and then in the brief space of a couple of minutes the whole mass with arms and baggage disappeared beneath the broken-up ice, not one man escaping or even appearing again at the top of the water. We looked down upon the churning, rippling waves produced by the struggles of so many human creatures swallowed up so suddenly, and a thrill of horror ran through us all.

Very soon the fractured ice, broken up by the useless efforts of those beneath it, sank again into repose, the clouds were once more reflected on its gleaming surface, and we knew that all was over. Much of the Russian artillery remained still harnessed at the edge of the waters or overturned in the ponds, and later it was melted down to form the Austerlitz Column set up in Paris in the Place Vendôme. Just as the waters closed over the last relics of the army which in the morning had all but surrounded us, the sun went down behind a mass of clouds on the horizon, snow began to fall very much as a curtain does after the last scene at a theatre, and the Emperor, Marshal Berthier, Marshal Soult, their various staffs, and I set off to find a shelter from the bitter cold of the night, making our way with the greatest difficulty through the dense darkness amongst the dead, the wounded, and the prisoners, of whom there were an immense number.

On the vast battlefield, which was many miles in extent, there was but one little shelter, the posthouse where travellers changed horses on the Olmütz road. The small amount of space in it was crowded with wounded, and I passed the night on the snow under an apple tree in the garden without fire or so much as a wisp of straw. It was intensely cold though the day had been so fine, but I counted myself lucky, and I was indeed a thousand times more fortunate than the 20,000 poor wretches lying out on the ground not far from me, all wounded, many dying, without fires and quite unattended.

Our prisoners told us that when our cavalry charge reached the gates of Austerlitz, the Russian and Austrian Emperors Alexander I. and Francis II. were looking down upon the battle from the castle. We should have been doubly venturesome had we known that a few more sabre cuts might have won us so costly a prize as these two crowned heads. It was this circumstance which led to the Battle of Austerlitz being also called that of the three emperors.

I was ordered to make a topographical survey of the battle field, and I also made sketches of the chief points of interest, writing on them the most remarkable incidents which had occurred at each spot. On the fifth day, as I was crossing the bloodstained battle field covered with the dead, I came upon a group of fourteen Russians, who when wounded had crawled close to each other for the sake of warmth. Twelve were already dead, but two still lived, their hollow cheeks, furrowed with the tears they had shed, bearing witness to the agony they had endured.

They made touching signs to me, entreating me to help them. I at once fetched some peasants from Soloknitz, and made them carry the poor fellows to a place of security. No words could describe the radiancy of their looks when they found that they were being lifted on to the rough stretchers of branches the peasants had made. One of them, who knew but one word of French, kept on repeating, '*Monsieur, monsieur!*' I put them under the care of our surgeons, and rejoined the emperor at Vienna. Before he left the army, he gave many of us rewards for our behaviour in the field, and I was made captain of a battalion of engineers.

I returned to France by way of Bavaria, and passing again through Munich I had the honour of being received by the King of Bavaria, who loaded me with favours. I had known him since I was a mere child at Strasburg, where he had been colonel of a French regiment.

He would not let me leave Munich till he had taken me to see the brothers Senefelder, who had just invented the art of lithography. The results obtained by them appeared to me incredible, and they wished me to try my hand at the work. I stopped with them for some hours, and made a sketch with their crayons on one of their stones. I then left them, and an hour later, to my great surprise, they sent the stone to me with twenty impressions of my design.

I took these proofs with me to Paris, and showed them to the emperor, who at once recognised the immense value of the invention, and he told me to follow it up, but I found very few people disposed to aid me, and other affairs soon called me away. It was not until 1812 that lithography was really introduced into France, and began to yield far better results than those achieved by the original inventors. I had the honour of bringing the first specimen into France, but it was the talented Madame la Comtesse de Molien, wife of the Minister of the Treasury, who was the first to make generally known the great value of the invention.

We were hardly back in Paris before the *fêtes* began celebrating the successes of the campaign of 1805; but fresh preparations were being made for war, and my painting was again and again interrupted by the various missions entrusted to me. I had to take orders from the major-general to the various corps the emperor was collecting in Bavaria and Saxony to oppose the King of Prussia, whose army was already formidable and prepared to attack. On October 9 the Prussians commenced hostilities at Schleitz by attacking the cavalry of Prince Murat. On the 10th Marshal Lannes took thirty pieces of cannon. In one of the charges of this eventful day Prince Louis of Prussia, nephew of the king, was killed by a sabre cut.

On the 12th Marshal Davout took possession of eighteen pontoon bridges ready for use.

On the 13th the armies continued to approach each other in order of battle at right angles, and in the evening the plain of Jena appeared to be perfectly encircled with the watchfires of the two or three hundred thousand Prussians who rested in security, confident in their vast numbers.

The fires of the French Army, on the other hand, hidden by the irregularities of the ground, were scarcely visible, and the apparent distance of the enemy still further encouraged the confidence of the Prussians. The night was fine and calm, and from the heights we occupied on the plateau above the plain of Jena the view of the illuminated camp below was magnificent. We felt as if we were preparing for a brilliant fete on the morrow, and the sentinels on either side chatted together at their outposts without any inclination to fight, as if in time of peace.

On October 14, 1806, just before sunrise a thick fog came on and wrapped the whole district in gloom for several hours. The emperor wished to turn the darkness to account by delaying the action long enough to allow our reserves and cavalry to come up, but the impatience of our troops led to the outposts opening fire on the enemy about nine o'clock. The whole line followed the movement, emerging through wide openings cleared and tested beforehand under Marshal Lannes.

The Prussians were also anxious to wait till the fog cleared away, but our attack roused them from their inaction, and their whole line also began to manoeuvre, changing front and marching upon Jena on their left. About eleven o'clock we could see their infantry advancing and deploying with precision, whilst their artillery arrived at a gallop at the head of an immense body of cavalry. When the two armies, marching towards each other, were nearly within musket shot, the 800 Prussian and French cannon simultaneously opened fire and exchanged salvoes. The thunder of the terrible discharge dispersed the fog, and soon nothing intercepted the rays of the sun but the smoke, which reproduced above the heads of the combatants the ranks in which they stood.

The whole army then engaged, and for some time the struggle was indecisive; but the emperor, hearing that Marshal Ney and a portion of Murat's cavalry had come up, ordered a general attack. The shock was terrible. The Prussian cavalry in their furious charge shattered themselves upon our bayonets, and our grape shot and cavalry completed their destruction. The Prussian divisions were mingled in a confused mass, in which every ball from our guns struck down some hundred victims, whilst the forces of the enemy were divided.

General Rüchel fled towards our left wing, and the King of Prussia turned towards Magdeburg.

The fall of night put an end to the fighting, but not to the pursuit of fugitives, and the victories of Jena and of Auerstädt, which Marshal Davout won the same day, left in our hands 200 flags with the black eagle, more than 40,000 prisoners, 500 pieces of artillery, with the baggage, pontoon trains, and stores of the Prussians, who left 30,000 dead upon the field, with an immense number of wounded.

The King of Prussia himself was wounded, as were also the two Dukes of Brunswick, the elder (who had made war on us in Champagne) so seriously that he died a few days later. Prince

Henry, brother of the King, Prince Hohenlohe, the Marshal von Mollendorff, General von Tauenzin, General Rüchel, and thirty other superior officers, were either killed or wounded, and in consequence of this terrible defeat the whole of Prussia as far as the Vistula fell into our hands in a few days.

The Grand Duchess of Brunswick, sister of Frederick the Great, was then living in a *château* near Potsdam, and I was sent to carry to her the respectful greetings of Napoleon, and to offer on his behalf to do her any service in his power. This princess, her heart wrung with the terrible disasters which had overtaken the kingdom so much aggrandised by her brother, was also grieving bitterly over the loss of her husband and her nephew Prince Henry, both killed at Jena. Still Her Royal Highness controlled her emotions in a wonderful way, received me kindly, expressed her gratitude to the emperor for his magnanimity, but asked only to have some of her property secured to her, and would not allow me to leave with her the guard of honour I had orders to place at her disposal.

Following up our successes we stopped for a few days at Posen, and the *grandees* of Poland came to do homage to the Emperor in their Oriental costumes. The contrast of the costly robes, the valuable furs, and the richly decorated weapons of the nobles with the wretched garments of the peasants, and the difference between the noble dignified bearing of the masters and the abject demeanour of the serfs, impressed me painfully, and the state of things in Poland was quite a revelation to me. The castles of the nobles with their gorgeous internal decorations were surrounded with rough huts, the thatched roofs tumbling to pieces, beneath which serfs and domestic animals such as pigs and poultry were huddled together in misery, protected but little from the weather.

Vast stretches of sand, here and there sparsely cultivated, alternating with gloomy pine forests, with the tumbledown huts void of all comforts for the inmates, gave to the country such a desolate poverty-stricken appearance, that our soldiers, used to their fair land of France, said to each other with a smile, 'They call this a country, do they? A fine country it is, too, where if you ask for bread (*kleba*) the only answer you get is *gué gué gué* (I haven't got any), or if you ask for water, you are told *zara zara* (presently). It's not our idea of a country, anyhow.'

A Pole brought up in the midst of such privations at once becomes a hero in war. The *moujik*, bent with toil and huddled beneath his sheepskin fastened at the waist with a rope of straw, becomes a spirited horseman as soon as he dons the plumed *schapska* and brandishes his lance with its floating pennon. His horse from the desolate Ukraine, which in his winter gear, with his long flowing mane reaching almost to the ground, seems crushed by the weight he carries, now holds himself up proudly, not a whit less ready for the battle field than his master. The Poles received us with enthusiasm as brothers and liberators. They were aided to form regiments, very soon 10,000 joined our army, and the emperor picked out a corps of the best of them to join his own guard.

What struck us most in the big town of Warsaw was that everywhere in the streets, the promenades, and the salons, we heard French spoken as perfectly as in Paris.

The memory of the terrible Suvoroff was still recent. That general had burnt half the city of Warsaw, and destroyed with his artillery its finest buildings, without being able to make the inhabitants open their gates. He was also cruel enough to have the whole population of Praga, a suburb on the left bank of the Vistula, massacred in the night without distinction of age or sex. The people of Warsaw looked upon us as the avengers of Suvoroff's atrocities. Kosciuszko, the valiant defender of the independence of Poland, had found consolation for his woes in our ranks.

There was but one sentiment with regard to the Russians, and no matter with whom we conversed the same opinions were expressed in excellent French. The ladies of Warsaw were as eager for our success as were their husbands and brothers, and so great was their sympathy for France that when, in 1813, six years later, Austrian troops occupied Warsaw, and the general in command, the Archduke Ferdinand, invited the ladies to a *fête* given by him, they all declined to go. The prince, irritated by their contempt, sent them an invitation to a second *fête*, giving them to understand that he would punish those who did not attend it.

This time they went, but they were all dressed in mourning, and none of them would dance, each one pleading as an excuse that she had lost a brother or some other relative in the war. Many of these ladies were very beautiful, with fair complexions and good figures; they were, moreover, as graceful as the Creole women so often are. Their lively yet dignified manners, and cordial reception of us, led us to hope for a pleasant winter in their society, but more serious matters than balls quickly summoned us elsewhere.

Prince Poniatowski, nephew of the last King of Prussia, had awaited our coming in his palace at Warsaw, and he now eagerly placed himself at the head of the Poles who had taken service under our Emperor. General Dombrowski, another Pole, was already in command of a French division. The French army crossed the Vistula on December 18 and 19, 1806, whilst the Russians were advancing in force to the support of their allies the Prussians.

Amongst the dense forests of pines, where we sank knee deep in the miry soil, we again came across the Cossacks, Kalmucks, Khirgesses and Tartars from the Ural districts, with whom we had first made acquaintance at Austerlitz a year ago.

We found the Russians at Pultusk and Golymin, and the Augereau and Davout divisions were there engaged in a fierce struggle. The miry nature of the ground added to the horrors of the combat. The Russian loss was very great. The luckless wounded had not the strength to drag themselves out of the mud to join their comrades in retreat, and were ridden down and crushed beneath their own artillery and that of the French in pursuit. No efforts, however strenuous, on the part of the teams of horses could enable them to drag their loads through the quagmire, soaked with blood and made up of the flesh of thousands of victims kneaded with the mire into a revolting mass which clogged the wheels, and the Russians were compelled to abandon all their artillery, including ninety cannon.

A great number of prisoners also fell into our hands. Marshals Lannes and Davout carried off the chief honours of the day (December 26, 1806). The next morning, when we were awaiting the signal for departure, my comrades asked me to make a sketch on the wall of the room we were in of some episode of the recent struggle in the town. They pointed a few bits of charcoal for me, and I sketched a dozen men and horses, the size of life, choosing some of the mounted Cossacks, whose quaint appearance had struck me and who had deafened us with their yells whilst they riddled us with their arrows. My companions, delighted with the faithfulness of the representation, scribbled the name of the artist at the bottom of the drawing, but the trumpet call to mount sounded before I could finish it.

The Pole who owned the house set store on this souvenir of the French, preserved it carefully, and changed the sign of his inn to that of the 'French Cossacks.' Thirty-three years afterwards some young Polish refugees whom I met at Toulouse recognised my name through having seen it beneath the picture on the wall of the inn at Pultusk. My more serious works will probably not last as long as the sketch, which has brought so much custom to this Polish inn.

During the night of the following day, I had orders to summon the Legrand division in all haste to cut off the retreat of a fugitive corps. The snow was falling, and it was pitch dark. I had no guide and nothing to direct me through the pine forests and over the quagmires, but fortunately the latter were now frozen over and pretty firm. I had been wandering vaguely about with no idea of my bearings for some two hours, when I came upon the bivouac of a few *chasseurs* of the guard who had lost their way.

Waiting for light, they were cooking the results of a little foraging in a big saucepan; some rice, a few fowls, and a goose or two, all boiled down together, had produced a most inviting hotch-potch, seasoned with such an appetite as it is not given to the great ones of the earth to know. The brave fellows invited me to share their supper, and my portion of their stew renovated my forces, exhausted by fatigue.

After a halt of a few minutes only, I resumed my search, and

I had gone about a mile when I heard some luckless Frenchman shouting, swearing, and calling for help. He and his horse were sinking in a bog, the ice on the top having broken beneath their weight. I was only able to approach with difficulty, for my horse refused to advance on such treacherous ground. But I thought I recognised the voice, and shouted, 'Who is it?'

The answer came back, 'It's you, Lejeune, is it? I am in the greatest danger. My horse has sunk to the neck, and I am lip to the waist in mud. I am exhausted with my struggles and benumbed with cold; for pity's sake get me out of this terrible pit. I shall be swallowed up directly.' It was General Legrand, the very man I was looking for, but, like myself, he was also ignorant what had become of his men and in peril of his life.

Not being able to fasten up my horse, and fearing to lose him, I wrapped his head up in my cloak, and thus blinded he remained perfectly still. I then approached the general on foot, and our combined efforts at last resulted in his getting to *terra firma*, whilst his horse, relieved of the weight of the rider, managed to get out of the mud. We then went off to try and find the lost division. First, we made out a few scattered fires, and then came upon the infantry, which were able to reach at daybreak the point to which I had orders to take them. The enemy in retreat had had no better road than we, and after defending them for some time they abandoned to us a good many pieces of cannon which had stuck in the mud.

General Legrand, whom I had just rescued from danger, was a fine fellow some six feet high, with a manly presence and a somewhat imperious manner, but a noble character. A little later he married General Scherer's daughter, who was perhaps the prettiest girl in Paris. She was the very ideal of a heroine of romance, such as the old chroniclers loved to paint. Her light golden hair floated from a dainty head set upon a charming figure, and resembled the fleeting mists which gather about the rising sun, and exhale in the morning air the scent of the flowers they have caressed during the night.

The stern and dignified warrior with his strong athletic limbs, yielding so gently and submissively to the lightest whim of his young bride, was like a new Hercules bound and conquered by love. The emperor liked his generals to marry, and often aided with liberal gifts to bring about unions which would otherwise have been difficult if not impossible.

We pursued the Russians through the forests for several days, but there was no fighting except a little skirmishing on the part of the advanced guard. The emperor then halted a few days to reorganise the army, which was much exhausted with the long struggle, and our headquarters were in a stable at Golymin, where we were all crowded together on the straw. Our privations did not at all damp our spirits, and one evening the emperor and Prince Berthier stopped a few minutes to hear us sing airs from the latest operas of Paris.

ALSO FROM LEONAUR
AVAILABLE IN SOFTCOVER OR HARDCOVER WITH DUST JACKET

THE FALL OF THE MOGHUL EMPIRE OF HINDUSTAN *by H. G. Keene*—By the beginning of the nineteenth century, as British and Indian armies under Lake and Wellesley dominated the scene, a little over half a century of conflict brought the Moghul Empire to its knees.

LADY SALE'S AFGHANISTAN *by Florentia Sale*—An Indomitable Victorian Lady's Account of the Retreat from Kabul During the First Afghan War.

THE CAMPAIGN OF MAGENTA AND SOLFERINO 1859 *by Harold Carmichael Wylly*—The Decisive Conflict for the Unification of Italy.

FRENCH'S CAVALRY CAMPAIGN *by J. G. Maydon*—A Special Correspondent's View of British Army Mounted Troops During the Boer War.

CAVALRY AT WATERLOO *by Sir Evelyn Wood*—British Mounted Troops During the Campaign of 1815.

THE SUBALTERN *by George Robert Gleig*—The Experiences of an Officer of the 85th Light Infantry During the Peninsular War.

NAPOLEON AT BAY, 1814 *by F. Loraine Petre*—The Campaigns to the Fall of the First Empire.

NAPOLEON AND THE CAMPAIGN OF 1806 *by Colonel Vachée*—The Napoleonic Method of Organisation and Command to the Battles of Jena & Auerstädt.

THE COMPLETE ADVENTURES IN THE CONNAUGHT RANGERS *by William Grattan*—The 88th Regiment during the Napoleonic Wars by a Serving Officer.

BUGLER AND OFFICER OF THE RIFLES *by William Green & Harry Smith*—With the 95th (Rifles) during the Peninsular & Waterloo Campaigns of the Napoleonic Wars.

NAPOLEONIC WAR STORIES *by Sir Arthur Quiller-Couch*—Tales of soldiers, spies, battles & sieges from the Peninsular & Waterloo campaigns.

CAPTAIN OF THE 95TH (RIFLES) *by Jonathan Leach*—An officer of Wellington's sharpshooters during the Peninsular, South of France and Waterloo campaigns of the Napoleonic wars.

RIFLEMAN COSTELLO *by Edward Costello*—The adventures of a soldier of the 95th (Rifles) in the Peninsular & Waterloo Campaigns of the Napoleonic wars.

AVAILABLE ONLINE AT **www.leonaur.com**
AND FROM ALL GOOD BOOK STORES

ALSO FROM LEONAUR
AVAILABLE IN SOFTCOVER OR HARDCOVER WITH DUST JACKET

THE 9TH—THE KING'S (LIVERPOOL REGIMENT) IN THE GREAT WAR 1914 - 1918 by Enos H. G. Roberts—Mersey to mud—war and Liverpool men.

THE GAMBARDIER by Mark Severn—The experiences of a battery of Heavy artillery on the Western Front during the First World War.

FROM MESSINES TO THIRD YPRES by Thomas Floyd—A personal account of the First World War on the Western front by a 2/5th Lancashire Fusilier.

THE IRISH GUARDS IN THE GREAT WAR - VOLUME 1 by Rudyard Kipling—Edited and Compiled from Their Diaries and Papers—The First Battalion.

THE IRISH GUARDS IN THE GREAT WAR - VOLUME 1 by Rudyard Kipling—Edited and Compiled from Their Diaries and Papers—The Second Battalion.

ARMOURED CARS IN EDEN by K. Roosevelt—An American President's son serving in Rolls Royce armoured cars with the British in Mesopatamia & with the American Artillery in France during the First World War.

CHASSEUR OF 1914 by Marcel Dupont—Experiences of the twilight of the French Light Cavalry by a young officer during the early battles of the great war in Europe.

TROOP HORSE & TRENCH by R.A. Lloyd—The experiences of a British Lifeguardsman of the household cavalry fighting on the western front during the First World War 1914-18.

THE EAST AFRICAN MOUNTED RIFLES by C.J. Wilson—Experiences of the campaign in the East African bush during the First World War.

THE LONG PATROL by George Berrie—A Novel of Light Horsemen from Gallipoli to the Palestine campaign of the First World War.

THE FIGHTING CAMELIERS by Frank Reid—The exploits of the Imperial Camel Corps in the desert and Palestine campaigns of the First World War.

STEEL CHARIOTS IN THE DESERT by S. C. Rolls—The first world war experiences of a Rolls Royce armoured car driver with the Duke of Westminster in Libya and in Arabia with T.E. Lawrence.

WITH THE IMPERIAL CAMEL CORPS IN THE GREAT WAR by Geoffrey Inchbald—The story of a serving officer with the British 2nd battalion against the Senussi and during the Palestine campaign.

AVAILABLE ONLINE AT **www.leonaur.com**
AND FROM ALL GOOD BOOK STORES

www.ingramcontent.com/pod-product-compliance
Lightning Source LLC
Chambersburg PA
CBHW021004090426
42738CB00007B/651